Sidney D. Drell

At SLAC, in front of chalkboard with equations, 1980:
beloved pedagogue, the calculus of physics his elegant
lingua franca of precision.

Sidney D. Drell

*Into the Heart of Matter,
Passionately*

Lenora Ferro
with Susan Southworth

HOOVER INSTITUTION PRESS

Stanford University | Stanford, California

With its eminent scholars and world-renowned library and archives, the Hoover Institution seeks to improve the human condition by advancing ideas that promote economic opportunity and prosperity, while securing and safeguarding peace for America and all mankind. The views expressed in its publications are entirely those of the authors and do not necessarily reflect the views of the staff, officers, or Board of Overseers of the Hoover Institution.

hoover.org

Hoover Institution Press Publication No. 714

Hoover Institution at Leland Stanford Junior University, Stanford, California 94305-6003

First printing 2020
26 25 24 23 22 21 20   7 6 5 4 3 2 1

Manufactured in the United States of America
Printed on acid-free, archival-quality paper

Library of Congress Cataloging-in-Publication Data
Names: Ferro, Lenora, author. | Southworth, Susan (Susan Elizabeth), author.
Title: Sidney D. Drell : into the heart of matter, passionately / Lenora Ferro ; with Susan Southworth.
Other titles: Hoover Institution Press publication ; 714.
Description: Stanford, California : Hoover Institution Press, Stanford University, 2020. | Series: Hoover Institution Press publication ; no. 714 | Includes bibliographical references and index. | Summary: "Examines the life and legacy of Sidney D. Drell, award-winning nuclear physicist, national security expert, behind-the-scenes diplomat, and champion for peace, disarmament, and human rights"-- Provided by publisher.
Identifiers: LCCN 2020030769 (print) | LCCN 2020030770 (ebook) | ISBN 9780817924041 (cloth) | ISBN 9780817924065 (epub) | ISBN 9780817924072 (mobi) | ISBN 9780817924089 (pdf)
Subjects: LCSH: Drell, Sidney D. (Sidney David), 1926-2016. | Nuclear physicists—United States--Biography. | Nuclear weapons--Government policy—United States—History. | Nuclear disarmament--United States--History. | LCGFT: Biographies.
Classification: LCC QC774.D74 F47 2020 (print) | LCC QC774.D74 (ebook) | DDC 530.092 [B]--dc23
LC record available at https://lccn.loc.gov/2020030769
LC ebook record available at https://lccn.loc.gov/2020030770

To my family—my Baron Brignand as favorite sidekick—
each with the trusty support I couldn't have done without,
and to the many others who also humble and inspire me.

—*Lenora Ferro*

Contents

Foreword

George P. Shultz

To me, Sid is a living memory, keeping me company even in his physical absence. I think often of the two of us, in his Hoover office or mine, discussing this idea or that, planning events to advance whatever cause we were advocating or composing a position paper on some matter of national concern for eventual publication.

One hope I now harbor for this book—an informal but extensive compilation of Sid's remarkable life history and highlights as related either in his own words or those of his loved ones, closest friends, colleagues, and allies—is that it will begin to awaken public attention to recognize and acknowledge this brilliant scientist who gave his broad-gauged talents to benefit some of the most important developments in the twentieth century, nationally and worldwide. Whether launching and mentoring generations of physicists, working on important secret government projects with the Jasons, fighting for justice for Russian physicist Andrei Sakharov, or advancing national and international security vis-à-vis nuclear weapons safety and nonproliferation, Sid was a welcome asset to any endeavor he undertook.

It was Sid's integrity coupled with his reliable and trustworthy ability to be diplomatic but also to be a fierce advocate for everything he valued that made him the all-around go-to guy I wanted with me at Hoover. Now his legacy rests with us. But it also must be revived as the exemplary and inspiring guidance that is so desperately needed in these times of uncertainty and divisiveness.

As you enjoy this walk through the highlights of Sid's distinguished but balanced lifetime and acquaint yourself with his multifaceted achievements, you'll hear the voices of many whose vivid memories bring Sid to full life. All of them, myself included, laud this opportunity to be part of spreading the word of this outsider's insider (as he referred to himself in the political and policy-making worlds) working behind the scenes.

Candidly told as his history is here, the stories are grounded in historical accuracy resulting from extensive research, while the voices of Sid himself and those who loved and admired him reveal the profound influence he contributed to society.

I offer my gratitude to the two whom Sid chose to author this informal history: my dear friend and assistant, Susan Southworth, as editor and researcher, along with writer Lenora Ferro, who penned this work of art. Both devoted years to its fruition, thriving on their own admiration for Sid as they composed this unique labor of love.

Preface

When Sidney Drell died, age ninety, at his home in Palo Alto, California, he left behind a legacy grand and influential enough to encompass three lifetimes. Drell excelled as a professor of physics, a theoretical physicist, a national security expert, an amateur musician, a behind-the-scenes diplomat, a champion for peace and human rights, and a husband, father, and mentor. He was a passionate man, although passions did not rule him. He was a humanitarian, gentle and sweet natured, though he could be a formidable foe when principle dictated. As a scientist, he was rigorous, incisive, and driven by curiosity and facts.

In anticipation of this book, he provided a list of contributors we could contact for interviews he felt would be helpful in telling his life's story. Initially a bit reluctant to "make a big deal" of his history, Sid grew increasingly enthusiastic (and expansive) as we reported back the extraordinary and highly relevant tales resulting from the interviews conducted. As his reluctance to be lauded waned and he began to recognize that this endeavor might also prove to be a contribution to posterity, his list of contributors grew—daily, at times—and he handed over to us a vast collection of documents, personal reflections, and memorabilia from family members, friends, and scores of acquaintances. Originally intended as a tribute to Drell on his ninetieth birthday, meant to be distributed among his friends and family, this publication has been expanded and reorganized to introduce a great man to a wider audience. As most of the interviews were conducted while Drell was still alive, we have maintained the present

Sidney Drell in his SLAC office: a man in his element, c. 1990.

tense in which they were offered or recorded in order to capture the spirited immediacy of the contributors' interactions with Drell.

Drell himself sat for many interviews; thus, his words grace much of the material included herein. Many other people also spoke or wrote at length about their admiration and respect for Drell and the ways in which he enriched their lives. Although the resulting collection contains elements of both biography and autobiography, the mixture bestows multifaceted lenses that present vistas of a man of many passions and talents, as seen through different eyes and perspectives—his own and those of family, friends, colleagues, and compatriots.

Drell represents an American experience now becoming all too rare. He combined academic excellence with government service in ways that complemented both. As a student, a professor, and then as a top-notch theoretical physicist, he was welcomed into the rarefied atmosphere surrounding those who split the atom and otherwise ushered in the nuclear age. And thereafter, as a humanitarian and scientist who could fully comprehend the consequences of the age's potentially world-shattering weapons, he devoted much of his life to the pursuit of nuclear sanity through advocacy for disarmament and nonproliferation. He liked to remind us that he stood on the shoulders of greats past as he pursued various opportunities to be of service in different arenas.

As a member of numerous advisory groups to the federal government, Drell was often in touch with the leading proponents of controversial actions, many of whom held widely differing perspectives. Integrity and civility were key Drell attributes that served to foster, facilitate, and maintain relationships with others in these various spheres, encouraging and enabling each of the participants to listen and learn from the others. Drell's reputation set a rare gold standard that welcomed him as a trustworthy affiliate to any effort or cause within his wide range of expertise.

Since the sundry elements of Drell's eclectic life overlap, separating the accounts of each into chapters posed a difficult task. His career as a physicist often intersected with his avocation as a violinist; his government service touched his family life; and his academic pursuits frequently accorded with his humanitarian instincts. As is evident in the reflections from others included here, the diverse realms of Drell's endeavors and interests were essentially intersecting circles inviting and accommodating the enrichments of cross-fertilization.

A brief look at various aspects of Drell's life, from family pets and traditions to national awards and his readiness to mentor students and inspire other musicians, reveals a man who combined an exceptional mind with a strong devotion to public service and a fondness for camaraderie, seasoned with a sense of humor and a frosting-on-the-cake humility that truly great people like Drell demonstrate.

Sid Drell was a brilliant man, a scholar of the highest order. Sincere and dynamic, his curiosity was vast, fed by his scientific work and complemented by forays into language, music, literature, philosophy, poetry, history, and art. Yet he was also "Sid, *just* Sid" to any and all.

Drell was keen to hone his abilities in order to apply them to best purpose. He was open and generous, eager to share his knowledge and bonhomie. He was a gregarious schmoozer who made lasting connections with people of all backgrounds. No one could walk away from an encounter with him without feeling refreshed, edified, or validated.

Being from a family of immigrants, Drell understood that a life devoted to connecting with community, with a sense of belonging and a love of learning, offered the best chance for happiness. His greatest riches were embodied in those with whom he surrounded himself—his family, his friends and colleagues, his students. Because of his remarkable accomplishments and his lasting, wide-ranging influence, exerted to great effect in so many realms and inculcated in so many, Drell deserves a place in our collective history. And luckily for us (the universal *us*, that is), the footprints and example Drell left to follow and emulate are part of the legacy he amassed in his inimitable ways. As such, these gifts have come to shape a culture and an ethos for generations of future scientists. Recognizing their duty to the greater good through scientific advancement and by worthy example, these qualitative and quantitative empiricists who follow in Drell's footsteps are empowered to guide us forward at a time when leadership from their various fields could not be more essential for society and for Mother Earth.

Phil Taubman, in his book *The Partnership*, offered the first scholarly treatment of Drell's life, focusing on his nuclear disarmament efforts with Henry Kissinger, Sam Nunn, Bill Perry, and George Shultz. It is the considered opinion of those who had the privilege of connection with Sid that, though he had his share of attention in the press, a great deal more is needed if his lifetime story is to receive the acclaim it deserves. This informal yet inclusive tribute was initiated to fill that void and perhaps invite greater recognition through broader exposure for one so deserving.

The array of "Sid stories" is intentionally *not* given a scholarly treatment here; instead we chose a style in keeping with the tone and overall approach Sid requested. Distinctively familiar in language, it also lends itself to Drell's own congenial style and comports with the affable ease and open-hearted joy in each contributor's reflections—something that Sid likely sensed would be optimal for the teller as well. As a result, it is through memorably instructive experiences, recalled candidly by those who knew him best, that our chosen presentation attempts to capture the family man, the teacher and mentor, the friend and colleague, and the quietly but firmly present, in-the-background national and international hero. He was, after all, "Sid, *just* Sid," whose memory and influence abide now with all who were privileged to know him.

〰〰

CHAPTER 1

A Life of
Groundbreaking Achievement

S id Drell's early life and upbringing were in many ways represen-
tative of the children of immigrants who come to this country
determined to create a better life for themselves and for their families.
His parents were Russian Jews who left Ukraine for a new beginning
in America in the early twentieth century. Overcoming the language
barrier and social restrictions for Jews, they embraced their new
country, became successful in their careers, and instilled in their son
a deep respect for education and a belief in the importance of maintaining community and helping others.

Sidney David Drell was born in Atlantic City, New Jersey, on
September 13, 1926, to Rose (White) and Tully Drell. More than a
decade earlier, his parents had emigrated to the United States from
different parts of Ukraine where Russians of Jewish heritage had
been consigned. Rose came from Zhitomir, in the west, and Tully
from Ostropol, cities whose Jewish populations would later be wiped
out by the Nazis in 1942.

Arriving in the United States in 1912, Tully served in the US Army
during World War I and thereafter graduated from Pennsylvania
State University. He and Rose met in Philadelphia, where she was
seeking a teacher's degree at Temple University and Tully, who already
held a degree in chemical engineering from a Russian university,
was pursuing a degree in pharmacology at the Philadelphia College

Young Drell in front of his father's Reliable
Pharmacy, Atlantic City, New Jersey, where Sid
lent a hand from time to time, c. 1934.

of Pharmacy and Science. Because Russian credentials held no weight
in his adopted country, this was Tully Drell's practical way to establish new qualifications and find security in an eventual second career.
This resolution to the major problem of making a living was an
example of the intellectual flexibility and gritty perseverance passed
along from father to son. After his graduation, Tully and Rose mar-
ried and eventually settled in the White family home in Atlantic City.

Few opportunities to secure professional jobs were available to Jews then, but Tully managed to achieve success as a pharmacist. Rose experienced changes in work expectations, as well, because the German language had been eliminated from the US high school curriculum during World War I, and Rose—who had trained to teach the language at high school level—found herself teaching grade school instead.

At first, life in Atlantic City was comfortable for the Drells. Rose's father had opened a thriving dry goods store and then invested his savings in real estate. His holdings included four apartment buildings, one of which was pressed into service as the family's home—on the entirely respectable Victoria Avenue, not far from the tony streets represented on the Monopoly game board.

Unfortunately, Grandfather White (his original family name was Kaplan) experienced devastating financial losses during the Great Depression, eventually forfeiting all his apartment buildings. "I was aware of the losses and of the changes in circumstances that we, along with everyone else, were suffering," Drell recalled, acknowledging his perception at that time, although he was still a child in the 1930s.

Yet, Drell's resilient father, Tully, was able to make a success of his pharmacy and survive in business despite his generosity in filling prescriptions for customers who couldn't pay during those rough times. Of his father's kindness, Drell said, "It was a neighborhood pharmacy, and he felt a duty to his local community." It was yet another point of pride for his son to recall how Tully "was a very modest, happy man who never sought attention, and from whom I learned how normal it is to do what you want as best as you can without aspiring to be a big shot in the eyes of others." Describing his father as a gentle man, Drell borrowed from William Wordsworth, who defined "that best portion of a good man's life / His little, nameless, unremembered, acts / Of kindness and of love."[1]

---

1. "Lines Composed a Few Miles above Tintern Abbey," 1798.

A hike in Mother Nature's wild splendor of Point Lobos, the "crown jewel" of California's state parks, with ocean views: the perfect engagement setting, 1951.

With regard to religious tradition, Grandfather White was the only devout member of his immediate family. Still, Drell felt a need to honor his beliefs and heritage: "It was mostly for him that I went through with my bar mitzvah, despite the fact that he had died shortly before the ceremony was to take place, and I could have opted out."

The concession on Drell's part pleased his mother, who was involved in Reform Judaism and advocated for her son's completion of his bar mitzvah as a way to show respect for his grandfather's beliefs. So it was that for several months Drell met weekly with a rabbi, learning the Hebrew alphabet and preparing to read passages competently. His father, though, wasn't among the celebrants during the ceremony, choosing instead to stand at the entrance and be technically present. "As far as I know, my father had never entered a synagogue," Drell explained. "He had no use for religion, and I hewed to his influence."

Young Sidney began his college career at age sixteen as one of the few public school graduates to attend the private and prestigious Princeton University. Graduating from Princeton in 1946, Drell went on to the University of Illinois at Urbana-Champaign for graduate studies. There he plunged into theoretical physics, earning a master's degree in 1947 and a doctorate in 1949. One of Drell's close friends during those years was the late Charles Slichter, who became a professor at the University of Illinois and a world-renowned research scientist in the field of magnetic resonance. He described Drell as "a brilliant theoretical physicist who was at ease with all his gifts, and none of it ever went to his head." The two enjoyed a lifelong close relationship, each garnering historic acclaim for his respective professional accomplishments. Both Drell and Slichter were honored by the University of Illinois's Grainger College of Engineering with induction into its Hall of Fame in 2013.

But along with deep personal connections made at the University of Illinois, and even with the extraordinary tutelage of great mentors, Drell's most life-changing event during his years there involved not physics, but chemistry—of a sort—in that the introduction to Harriet Jane Stainback, a native of Minter City, Mississippi, deserved the honor of "best ever."

A String Quartet for Courtship

It was Easter week of 1949. Drell was busy writing his thesis when a friend stopped by to invite him to a party hosted by two female graduate students at their campus apartment. Drell was reluctant but eventually agreed to join him. Taking his "unshaved, unwashed, ill-dressed self," he brought along a package of jelly beans as "some sort of social contribution" to the party. Harriet, it turned out, was one of the event's hosts.

When Drell called on her a few days later, Harriet couldn't quite place him among the party guests, though she did accept his invitation to hear a concert of string quartets. Still, the offer held no special personal significance for Harriet, whose frank admission was that "my roommate and I always accepted invitations to dinner or to concerts during those times." (So, though Harriet had some assurance that this potential suitor Drell was no slouch or cad, it was the concert itself that tempted her sufficiently to accept.)

That musical evening marked the beginning of a relationship that would flourish for the next seven decades. Drell's friend Slichter recalled initiating together, soon thereafter, what would be "a day of special joy" when he and Drell spied Harriet as she was teaching a German class outdoors: "We decided that it was a perfect occasion for the two of us to entertain them all with a serenade. We were right about the opportunity being ideally timed: it was."

Sid and Harriet were well matched in many ways, not least of which was their love of learning and regard for academic achievement, threaded throughout their individual family histories. Born into a lineage of bibliophiles and all-around literati, Harriet offered some examples of their legacy as it was carried forward: "My mother and all of her siblings were very well educated. One of my aunts became a missionary and spent years in China; Aunt Persis had a PhD in statistics from Smith and worked at the Rockefeller Institute; and one of my uncles graduated from West Point." And though there were no bookstores in her small town when she was growing up, the absence posed no hindrance for Harriet: "Luckily, I received a steady supply of good books from my aunts."

Sid and Harriet's younger daughter, Joanna, emphasized how much both parents' families valued education: "It's family lore that our mother's great-aunt helped to put my grandmother and her sisters through college, an unusual accomplishment for women at the turn of the century, and my grandmother's brother went to West Point, so they all were byproducts of first-rate educations. The regard for learning on both sides of my family across generations and the example set by my parents ensured that education was front and center in our home."

At Wellesley, Harriet majored in German and spent a year abroad in Zurich. Her minor was Russian, with Vladimir Nabokov as one of her professors. She characterized him as a "charming man" whose wife, Vera, was the more accomplished teacher of the two and often substituted for him while he spent his time writing. Harriet then pursued graduate studies in German and picked up Russian again at the University of Illinois. No formal Russian courses were on offer then, but native speakers were enlisted to teach the few students who were interested. After receiving her master's degree in German in 1950, Harriet went to Washington, DC, where she taught Russian at the Armed Forces Security Agency (now the National Security Agency).

Meanwhile, after earning his doctorate in 1949 at the University of Illinois, Drell stayed on for another year as a postdoctoral student. Then, after a short stint at the government's nuclear complex in Oak Ridge, Tennessee, he accepted a position as physics instructor at Stanford in 1950. Soon after his arrival, he was greeted by the first of many opportunities to participate in government assignments— through John Wheeler, who had been Drell's senior thesis adviser at Princeton. The invitation concerned a secret project: the development of the hydrogen bomb. Drell declined the offer, choosing instead to remain in academia. (Fate would later call him back to work on weapons, though his goal would be limiting their number rather than developing them.)

In 1951, Drell traveled from Stanford to Washington for a conference of the American Physical Society. The main motivation for the trip, of course, was to visit Harriet, but despite the primary goal of a romantic diversion, he managed to produce a credible conference report. The couple reunited later that year when Harriet visited Palo Alto, and Drell recalled the happy moment during her stay when the two decided to marry.

Harriet was not Drell's only love, though. He had also "fallen in love with California," but he'd been offered a postdoctoral fellowship at the Massachusetts Institute of Technology that was tempting him as well. So in January 1952, he made the decision to leave Stanford for MIT, with Victor "Viki" Weisskopf as his adviser. The following year, when Weisskopf offered him a position on the MIT physics faculty, Drell readily accepted.

Sid and Harriet wed in March 1952 in a ceremony held at Harriet's childhood home in Minter City. In droll terms, Drell described the nuptials: "There was no music, no froth. Our wedding was very simple, as it should have been, because there were already enough things out of natural order down in Mississippi for Harriet to agree to marry me in the first place. After all, my family and I, with our Jewish heritage, were 'integrating' a family with deep roots to the Pilgrims on Harriet's mother's side, and on her father's side there were Southern roots about to be disturbed." Perhaps Harriet's unconventional ruby-red bridal gown was a talisman of the spirit attending the union of these two culturally distinctive but equally lively and strong-willed mates.

Slichter, who had become a close friend of the couple at the University of Illinois, attended the wedding and recalled it as "a fascinating event. Harriet is gentle, unassuming, and gracious, with lovely Southern manners, and the ceremony took place in her family home—a wonderful country estate in the Deep South, while Sid hails from Atlantic City and a family of very different heritage and background." Few in those days, with the exception of those who knew the couple well, would have expected such a successful and happy union.

Drell recalled an atmosphere of welcoming harmony from his in-laws, saying that he "was always at ease with Harriet's parents and relatives. There were never any undercurrents swirling or moments of awkwardness. Among the many fond memories are smoking cigars and drinking bourbon with Harriet's father."

Through the lens of family history, it appears that the official beginning of Sid and Harriet Drell's marriage accurately foreshadowed the

Wedding photo of Sid and Harriet, Minter City, Mississippi,
March 22, 1952. A simple ceremony but a complex
match . . . and a gown of unconventional crimson.

lifelong, contented union of two independent-minded and uniquely
endowed souls, joined together to nurture and honor separate selves.

Daughter Joanna described the influence of her parents' marriage
in this way: "The mutual respect my parents showed to each other is
what impressed me the most about their relationship. Although my
father climbed the heights of the scientific community, he always
welcomed my mother's influence. That sort of respect was not even

in question, which is how it should be, and it's something I try to emulate."

Indian Pudding Nights and Eggnog Sprees

In 1956, after four years at MIT, during which time the Drells' first two children were born, the family relocated to Stanford, where they purchased a stately house at 570 Alvarado Row. Built in 1892, the Queen Anne–style structure with its twin towers was so attractive that it was featured on campus postcards. Its first occupants were the German professor James O. Griffin, his wife, Bessie, and their black cat (also named Bessie).

Like the Griffin residents before them, the Drells welcomed feline companionship. "Cats were a constant presence in our home when the children were growing up," Harriet recalled. "Those who played the largest role in our children's lives were Harvard, Princeton, Ole Miss, and Wellesley, who will always be remembered by all of us. Joanna's beloved Rebound and Hoops even came to live with us for several years. And although our house was in the middle of the Stanford campus, we never lost a cat. They survived and thrived."

That the felines all survived and thrived may have been partly because the Drell children looked out for them—Joanna in particular. She reminisced about one family "cattums" tradition that she found dicey: "We always had cats. They were part of our family and added great spirit to our home. I resisted my parents' insistence on the nightly ejection of the cats into the outdoors. Still, it was hard to wrangle four cats in or out of a big house, and I admit to having felt guilty pleasure when one or more of them managed to evade the roundup."

Sid and Harriet were well known for their hospitality and their ways of creating a community of friends and acquaintances. Many happy and inspiring occasions took place at 570 Alvarado Row, including family meals around the kitchen table, casual and serious (and, at times, polemical) chats with Sid's students, lively chamber music sessions, and post–softball game picnics.

Persis, now Stanford's provost, remembers many of those occasions. "There were Indian pudding nights and eggnog parties—gatherings that are remembered fondly by friends who still talk about those events when I see them. Dad was a superb host with a delicate touch that tacitly invited guests into conversation."

There was always room for visiting friends and former students—or for current students in need of a temporary place to stay or even a quiet spot to roost while writing a thesis. A cherished destination, 570 Alvarado Row was a haven for intellectual sparring, growth, discourse, or rabble-rousing, for artistic reveries, refuge, or work—with Harriet as the ever-gracious hostess. Drell recalled interesting incidents in which Harriet's familiarity with the Russian language played a role:

In the early 1960s, we had a Russian visitor who stayed on the third floor of our home. Dr. A. A. Akhrem was a chemist from the Soviet Academy of Sciences in Moscow who was a visiting investigator in Stanford's chemistry department. At the time, Harriet was reading books in Russian but didn't speak the language fluently. When Akhrem showed up, he noticed a copy of *Doctor Zhivago*, in Russian, on open display in the living room, and offered his opinion to Harriet that "Pasternak is a great poet, but this is not a good book." Later, we noticed that, despite his criticism, he read that book again and again.

During Dr. Akhrem's stay, we had many evenings filled with captivating—and sometimes unusual—conversations. When Harriet's Russian teacher, Madame Kliatchkov, came for tea and met Dr. Akhrem, she felt obliged to lecture him on Khrushchev's "insult that brought shame on the Russian people"—referring to Khrushchev's shoe-table slamming at the United Nations General Assembly in 1960. Wisely, we left the two native Russians to their tense moments.

Joyce Kobayashi, a Stanford undergraduate when she first met the Drell family and now a psychiatrist in Denver, described the Drells as having raised their three children in a cherished old home with a backyard garden full of flowers where their children would often play while Harriet would relax with her book du jour. She remembered the setting as welcoming, like its hosts: "Their living room was simply adorned, very comfortable, and familiar to the many students and colleagues whom Sid would invite into their home."

Drell took seriously the care and feeding of his graduate students, often inviting them to dinner but not always remembering to give Harriet advance notice. Ashton Carter, who later served as secretary of defense under President Obama, admitted that, as one of Drell's hungry grad student visitors, he had more than once tried to wheedle an invitation to enjoy some of Harriet's home cooking.

The combination of the Drells' easy hospitality and the location of their home near the center of the Stanford campus, far removed from the "faculty ghetto" where younger faculty resided, made it a natural salon. The Drells' three children thus grew up in an atmosphere of academic exploration and the camaraderie it engendered.

Although now in a different location and used for offices, the Drells' home—site of so many of these memories—is still one of the most attractive buildings on campus. "Year by year," Drell recalled, "houses on Alvarado Row were taken down, but our house and another, the Owen House that was its mirror image on Salvatierra Way, remained." Now designated as historic buildings, both were moved to O'Connor Lane near the law school in 2005. "There was a hitching post near the front steps of our home that the university planned to discard when the house was moved," Sid said, "but Persis protested until they relented. The powers that be finally decided that since this house had historic status, the original hitching post should remain with it."

The Drell House on campus: a home, a hive of intellectual discourse, and a happy refuge sheltering many.

In the Family: Scientific Pursuits

Sid and Harriet's children, exposed not only to high-level physics but also to a wide range of disciplines and ideas in the Drell household, were emboldened by this freedom and intellectual curiosity to take their own individual paths. Daniel, the oldest, claimed he chose to major in biology partly in reaction to his father's emphasis on physics at the dinner table: "When our family would gather 'round the table for supper, my parents would ask, 'What did you do in school today?' After we'd taken our turns to answer, one of us would invariably pose the same question to our father, and out came the physics . . . which, of course, I couldn't understand. That's when the idea took root: Why not choose an area of science that would allow me to be as confusing to my father as he was to me when we talked about our professional lives?"

There were other, more objectively grounded reasons for Daniel's choice of biology as a profession, including the onset of juvenile diabetes at age eleven and the influence of a high school biology class taught by Robert Anderson. One morning in December 1967, Anderson asked Daniel's class members if they had seen the news that Christiaan Barnard, the South African surgeon, had performed the first human heart transplant. That, Daniel recalled, prompted Anderson "to throw the ongoing curriculum out the window and launch us, his students, into several weeks of modest explorations into immunology."

"With glass microscope slides, those horrific, little foil-wrapped lancets for finger pricks, and some anti-A and anti-B serum, he guided us as we blood-typed ourselves. By the end of those experiments, I'd decided that immunology was the most fascinating science there was. Then, in college, I met and eventually was invited to do graduate work with an immunologist, which led to my PhD degree in immunology." After thirty years of government service, Daniel retired in 2018 as the program manager of the Office of Biological and Environmental Research for the Department of Energy Joint Genome Institute.

In thinking about her path to a career aligned with her father's, Persis recalled many dinner conversations with guests, in particular physicist and Nobel Prize winner Richard Feynman.

A frequently visited memory is of someone sitting at our dinner table with us, students gathered in the living room with a distinguished visitor, or students convening at the kitchen table during the troubled times of the 1970s. Some other memorable times unfolded when Dad would host Richard Feynman. I would position myself in the shadows in the corner because I didn't want to go to bed; I just wanted to sit there and listen. It wasn't that Feynman was a prominent physicist; he was simply a charismatic person to watch. The conversation (not the actual content, but the idea of it) was always fascinating—in this case, doubly so because of the captivating guest.

And harking back to her middle school years, Persis remembered how, in seventh grade, she was initially tracked low in math. As she recalled those formative years:

My parents' reaction was to trust that the teachers would figure things out eventually. I worked hard to prove that the teachers were wrong, and a month later I was placed in the higher class. The end result was that I became very competitive in math. When I took physics in high school, it was dreadful, awful, appallingly bad. Even after I'd figured out, with my father's help, that the teacher had erred in an explanation during class, the teacher's reaction was, "Oh, yeah, you're right . . . but we won't tell the class because it's not important."

It was fortuitous that I missed the last quarter of that physics class. My father took a sabbatical in Rome that year, so from March onward I skipped school, I wrote papers for English and history, and I explored Rome.

And later, it wasn't always easy for Persis to be the physicist daughter of a very prominent physicist. "I got teased a lot about my father as I made my own way in the field. I remember 'Beer Can and Dull' as the insiders' witty nickname for the classic textbook that my father and 'bj' Bjorken wrote. By the way, volume one of Bjorken and Drell is a classic—beautifully, beautifully written."[2]

---

2. The book is by James D. Bjorken and Sidney D. Drell, *Relativistic Quantum Mechanics* (New York: McGraw-Hill, 1964).

Persis earned degrees at Wellesley and the University of California–Berkeley and joined the physics faculty at Cornell University. In 2002, she returned to Stanford as a professor and associate director of research at the Stanford Linear Accelerator Center (now called the SLAC National Accelerator Laboratory), eventually becoming director in 2007. She was named dean of the School of Engineering in 2014 and became Stanford's provost in 2017.

At a Stanford event, "What Matters to Me and Why," on May 4, 2016, Persis spoke to the apparent "father-daughter footsteps," clarifying the happenstance of striking similarities that she and Sid shared. She offered this explanation:

I did not set out to follow in my father's footsteps. Now, I will admit there are some superficial similarities that are hard to deny. He's a physicist; I'm a physicist. He's in high energy physics, but he's a theorist and I'm an experimentalist. He's at Stanford; I'm at Stanford. He was deputy director at SLAC; I was director at SLAC. He plays the violin; I play the cello. We play string quartets. We even play string quartets together. But actually, I didn't follow in his footsteps. It's just coincidence.

Persis added a scientist's spin on the coincidental likenesses, describing the two as akin to fermions. Specifically, it was the limiting characteristic of fermion particles—that they cannot occupy the same state as another particle of the same type—that Persis alluded to as the (mostly) contrasting quality in the Drells' father-daughter similarities. As she explained, "That quality speaks to the fact that the two of us, for all our years on the Stanford campus, were present together in the same place only three times."[3]

3. "What Matters to Me and Why—Sidney and Persis Drell," Stanford Humanities Center, Stanford University, May 4, 2016.

Music Appreciation: A Family Affair

The youngest Drell child, Joanna, is the only one who chose a career outside science, opting instead for medieval history. As father Drell recalled, "Harriet and I were delighted to have one child who is not a scientist but rather a medieval historian. It's a privilege to have a mix; but, to me, the vagaries of my children's careers, more or less successful, are not what matters. The measure is the integrity, intelligence, and strong bond to family that our children have, along with their eagerness to help when needs crop up. Another great source of happiness for us as parents is the fact that each of our children has made what we consider a beautiful marriage."

Today, Joanna is a specialist in medieval-Renaissance European history and chair of the University of Richmond's Department of History. (Both Joanna and her husband, David, also a medieval historian, are language lovers who speak fluent Italian.) Joanna attributes her complete freedom of educational and career choice primarily to her father's regard for her mother's background in the humanities. She was also constantly aware of the breadth of her father's life beyond physics.

At Wellesley, Joanna discovered two major passions: medieval history, thanks to the guidance of a great professor, and a cappella singing with the Wellesley Widows. While Daniel studied piano and violin and Persis is well known as a cellist, Joanna discovered her musical passion lay in singing. Her path to discovery, as she explained, wasn't an expected one.

"We grew up with poetry and maybe a little opera overkill," Joanna recalled. "I followed in Daniel and Persis's footsteps and studied piano with Hazelle Miloradovitch. But the piano didn't take the way it should have. My parents and Hazelle were a little startled by my enthusiasm for the Great American Songbook and classical musical theater in high school and college. Turns out I had secret 'diva' yearnings, and despite Dad's contrasting personal preferences, when I discovered singing, he couldn't have been prouder—even though my first big solo was a show tune."

Sid Drell explained how his affinity for music, as performer and listener, was rooted in childhood:

> We often had music in the house when I was growing up. My grandfather had a wind-up Victrola with the old green RCA Victor label. My father sang Russian music from time to time, and my mother loved to sing and accompany herself on the piano. So music was a presence in my formative years, but not until later did it become an essential part of my life.
>
> During those early years, I remember hearing songs sung by Caruso and a wonderful aria from Bizet's *The Pearl Fishers*. And though I heard a few operas in person, I had no exposure to chamber music. I took music lessons and played the violin in my high school orchestra, from which I was chosen to perform with the New Jersey State Orchestra.

The clarinet had been Drell's first instrument, but he switched to the violin, "probably because it was so popular during that Jascha Heifetz era." (Russian American Heifetz was a child prodigy considered by many as the greatest violinist of the twentieth century.) "But music wasn't a real force in my life until my senior year at Princeton, right after the war and just after I'd returned from a serious illness that sidelined me for several months. That spring, the Budapest String Quartet came to town and I went to hear them play. A whole world blew open! Until then, I thought that playing an instrument was something you did mainly to make your mother happy. Hearing the Budapest String Quartet perform the Beethoven cycle marked the beginning of my passion for music."

Drell took his violin to graduate school and started to play in a string quartet at the University of Illinois. "One Sunday night, I was practicing in my physics office when a stranger walked in and said,

'We need you in the orchestra.' That's how I came to play in the University of Illinois Orchestra for the four years I was there. The man who had walked by an open window and heard me scratching away was Robert Commanday, assistant professor of music at Illinois." Later, Commanday went on to a thirty-year career as music critic for the *San Francisco Chronicle*.

Drell described the music school at Illinois as a "fantastic place." There was a quartet in residence, the orchestra performed Handel's *Messiah* at the annual Christmas concerts, and Drell had the good fortune to play in performances conducted by Igor Stravinsky and Aaron Copland. "It was quite an experience to play *Jeu de cartes* under Stravinsky's direction."

While at the University of Illinois, Drell also learned to appreciate New Orleans jazz.

My friends and I would take the train to Chicago and visit one of our graduate school colleagues. He would put us up at his place and take us to joints on the South Side to hear real Dixieland jazz played by the likes of Muggsy Spanier.

Throughout my career, I've enjoyed playing music with many great physicists. During my first two years as an instructor at Stanford, I worked diligently on the Beethoven, Brahms, and Mozart sonatas with Felix Bloch, a good pianist and a Nobel Prize laureate.

When Drell made his way to MIT in 1952 to work with Viki Weisskopf, the two men often played violin-piano sonatas together. "Viki always teased me that he'd hired me mainly because Felix Bloch had told him I was a good violinist. I also enjoyed playing Brahms, Beethoven, Mozart, and Schubert sonatas with Francis Low, a theoretical physicist and professor at MIT who had taken part in the Manhattan Project. Low was one of my best friends during my years at MIT, and we crossed paths later as members of Jason."[4]

Returning to Stanford in 1956, Drell began playing string quartets regularly with Hazelle Miloradovitch, whom he had met during his earlier years at Stanford when both were members of the university's symphony orchestra. Miloradovitch became music teacher to the Drells' children and was a beloved figure in the Drell household. She harkened back to some vivid memories made there:

> [Sid Drell was] the most marvelous person and a very dear friend. Sid and I came independently to Stanford in the fall of 1951. I was a scholarship graduate student when friends who were playing in a string quartet with Sid introduced me to him. The group needed someone to fill in on violin one day, so I was recruited. That was the beginning of so very many years of happy chamber music sessions with Sid. Sid also played the violin in the Stanford orchestra under Sandor Salgo, as did I.
>
> After Sid and Harriet married and returned to Stanford in 1952, Harriet would listen to our chamber music group play. A true bibliophile, she would often stay for a while and then head off to read. Occasionally, our group included prominent physicists, one of whom was Felix Bloch. We also played with Leonard Schiff of the physics department, who was a fine musician on clarinet.

Because of his love for the violin, Drell wanted his son to play, too, so he asked Miloradovitch to give Daniel lessons. Miloradovitch recounted events of the early days in her long acquaintance with the family: "Daniel and I would be in the middle of a violin lesson when Persis, three years old at the time, would stand at the top of the landing on the big staircase and call down, 'I want to play the piano! I

---

4. Jason is a group of science advisers to the federal government and is described more fully in chapter 3.

want to play the piano!' So she began taking lessons with me and continued through high school. Persis was a very good student. Meanwhile, she independently took up the cello, which she continues to play in a string quartet."

Miloradovitch also recalled with delight the day that Joanna was born:

> Our chamber music group had gathered at the Drell house while Harriet was in the hospital. Sid received the call that Joanna had arrived . . . just as we were playing a string quartet. What an auspicious entry she made!
>
> At first, Joanna was a piano student of mine. Then, at the age of her bat mitzvah, Sid and Harriet gave her the choice of continuing or discontinuing her piano lessons. We had a meeting— Sid, Harriet, Joanna, and I—at the end of which Joanna opted not to continue with piano lessons. That was the end of an era of weekly visits to the Drells' house for music lessons. I remember crying all the way home!

Joanna had begun taking singing lessons by that time. "She had a powerful voice," Miloradovitch said, "akin to Sid's sonority and ability to project. When Sid, Harriet, and I attended a concert at Stanford and heard Joanna sing, we all felt proud."

A Quest for the Best Violin

Drell purchased the violin that he would keep for the rest of his life during the year he and his family spent in Geneva, where he worked at CERN, the European Organization for Nuclear Research, from 1961 to 1962.

> One of my former physics professors at Princeton, Josef Jauch, was teaching at the University of Geneva at the time and, upon discovering that I was at CERN, he contacted me. He played first

violin in a local quartet that was in need of a second violinist, so he invited me to join the quartet.

I was playing very well then, so I decided that I would look for a better violin. Pierre Vidoudez was a well-regarded luthier in Geneva who had a large inventory of fine violins, so I went to consult with him about finding a new instrument. My pocketbook limited my choice, but after trying many, I found a French violin that I liked. By this time, the International Conference on High Energy Physics was about to begin, and since I was one of the main speakers and had to concentrate on preparing my speech, I told Monsieur Vidoudez that I would have to delay my decision on purchasing the violin I favored until after the conference.

Who should show up at the conference but a colleague, Jack Fry, a physicist from the University of Wisconsin. He had become interested in analyzing the physics of the violin, his focus being the vibrations of the box for the low tones and the vibrations due to the F-holes for the higher tones. Fry had brought along a violin that he had made, and I found that I liked it much better—and it was less expensive—than the French violin I'd been considering. So I bought it right there and then.

When Drell showed the violin to Vidoudez, the luthier huffed disdainfully, "That's the work of an amateur." In his judgment, Drell's violin lacked the requisite polish and surface refinement. Sometime later, though, Vidoudez offered to trade one of his violins for Drell's, but Drell refused and defended his rightful decision: "My new violin wasn't polished, but it was a strong instrument. It was my violin, and I was happy with it. For decades, until a shoulder injury ended my music-making life, it served me beautifully."

Drell's musical life was dominated by quartets ever since his discovery of string quartet music at Princeton.

There's nothing like being part of an ensemble when you're clicking together—each musician playing with and for the group as well as for personal benefit. Our Stanford quartet never performed for an audience except on rare occasions when a member's spouse happened to attend a session. Otherwise, we played only for each other and for the pure pleasure of it.

Sandor Salgo, director of the Stanford orchestra, was always drafting me, and I played in the orchestra regularly until my Washington life interfered, beginning in 1960. The only time I played publicly in a quartet rather than as a member of an orchestra (where mistakes don't stand out!) was for one of the Sunday afternoon recitals in Cubberley Auditorium that Salgo frequently organized. It was 1952, and I remember playing second violin in Schubert's beautiful *Quartettsatz*, joined by a music professor who played the viola, a first violinist, and a cellist. Dorothy Nichols, a reporter for the *Palo Alto Times*, reviewed our performance. In that one and only review of my one and only public performance, she opined that we "showed that quartet playing is one of the most difficult arts and doesn't always come off." Some reviews I never forget!

Drell was as eager to applaud and promote other musicians as he was to perform himself. An example is his relationship with opera star Beverly Sills.

In 1965, Sid and Harriet attended a New York City Opera production of Mozart's *Don Giovanni* at Stanford's Frost Amphitheater. A little-known singer at the time, the soprano in the role of Donna Anna sang two arias in sufficiently ethereal legato and *squillo* for Drell to pronounce her a prima donna in the making: "I was blown out of my seat by this fantastic soprano and I said to myself, 'Wow, this kid's great! What's her name?'" It was Beverly Sills, and Drell predicted an illustrious future for her.

Drell continued to follow her rise in the opera world. A few years later, after Sills had fulfilled his prediction by making a name for herself, Drell decided to take in her performance in Rimsky-Korsakov's *Le coq d'or* while he was lecturing in New York City. He scheduled his classes accordingly, only to have the Met announce that Sills was unable to perform because she was making her debut at La Scala. For him, that was a shot of validation mixed with dismay.

In Erice, Sicily, 1975, taking a break from physics with his Jack Fry violin, an instrument Sid chose for a lifetime of sublime tone.

In his subsequent letter to Sills, a wounded Drell described his great disappointment. "I built my schedule in New York around hearing you, but when I got to the opera, you weren't there—you'd gone on to greater things." Sills wrote back and invited Drell to hear her in Massenet's *Manon* in San Francisco. Drell went backstage to meet her in person after the performance. Thereafter, friendly correspondence continued for a number of years—including a June 1974 letter in which Drell congratulated "DOCTOR Beverly Sills" after she received an honorary doctorate from Harvard.

Drell gave much thought to the correlation between music and science:

In physics, you've got to be rigorous about what nature does. It's a miracle that nature has these laws that we can understand.

It's a constant, beautiful structure, but it's limited. You're tied to the laws of nature when you do science. On the other hand, you're free when you perform or listen to music.

Music serves as a tremendous balance to our work in physics. No doubt that's why it plays such an important role in the lives of many scientists. In physics, as in all science, it is nature that speaks, but in music it is ourselves who speak as we conjure and bring to life the masters and their masterpieces.

For the Love of Literature

In addition to developing an appreciation for music as a child, Drell was introduced to a wide variety of good literature by his father. Drell read "the usual boys' books" and enjoyed stories by Joseph Conrad and Charles Dickens—*A Tale of Two Cities*, in particular. He also learned to appreciate poetry because of his father. "I remember the day he came home and presented me with a copy of Walt Whitman's *Leaves of Grass*." In fact, Drell kept his father's personal copy of Whitman's classic in his bookcase to his last days. But Drell got off to a rocky start with Shakespeare:

In my four years of high school, two years were spent with an English teacher who worked with great particularity on the details of *As You Like It*. I didn't like it! I was annoyed that I had to study it twice, and it still didn't impress me very much. So, on that basis I decided that I could do without that guy!

As a result, when I got to Princeton and was informed that Shakespeare was a required freshman course, I protested. I told my adviser that my high school teacher had damaged my enthusiasm for the Bard, and I pleaded, "Couldn't I, please, take an American literature course?"

Miracle of miracles, my adviser agreed, and it turned out to be a great course. My classmates and I learned about the excesses as well as the beauty in Whitman's writings, such as "When Lilacs Last in the Dooryard Bloom'd," "O Captain! My Captain!" and

"I Hear America Singing," and it was in that American literature course that I first read *Moby-Dick*, among other great works of literature. I also learned to appreciate Southern poetry. Quite early, too, I developed an affinity for George Bernard Shaw.

His love of literature, Drell liked to say, "broadened greatly after giving Shakespeare the cold shoulder." Later, during his teaching days at MIT, he ran across a statement in a student publication that resonated lifelong: "Hell, when a little Aristotle is mixed in with the Mechanics, the scientific and the humane are pretty well wedded. All we've got to agitate for is an early Spring."[5] That spirited attitude was one to emulate and pass along, as Drell did.

Drell's real expansion in reading came when he met the highly literate Harriet, who introduced him to many great books that had a lasting influence on him, such as Leo Tolstoy's *War and Peace* and Victor Hugo's *Les Misérables*—works, he said, "that are full of important social analysis." Harriet also drew him into the world of William Faulkner. Drell said of Faulkner, "His book *A Fable* is difficult to read, but it is powerful, its theme being that mankind will not only endure, but prevail."

Drell also admired Abraham Lincoln as a wordsmith:

One of the great reads of my life was the Library of America's collection of Lincoln's letters and speeches. He was a gifted writer, and his sentiments on any subject, from love to war to friendship, are touching. In my opinion, for all of his brilliant and beautifully written speeches and letters—some of which he sent to children whose fathers had been lost in service—Lincoln merits mention as one of America's great literary figures.

These habits of mind and spirit—lessons and indulgences in music, in language, and in literature—have significantly affected

---

5. Vinay Ambegaokar, *Voo Doo, M.I.T. Humor Monthly* 38, no. 1 (February 1955).

my professional life, in addition to being influential in my personal life. Our exposure to the arts and our experiences with them also serve as subjects of great and stimulating conversations and engender creative bonds in relationships. The arts have contributed in immeasurable ways to the quality of my life, and those influences have colored the lives of our children and grandchildren, as well.

In addition to sharing his passion for music, Drell imparted his love of literature to his children. Joanna remarked on how she was influenced deeply by her father's literary interests:

I knew that Dad loved poetry, with Robert Frost a favorite. It was at the beginning of my sophomore year in college that I became acutely aware of Dad's degree of fatherly love, poetically speaking, after I suffered my first heartbreak.

I was at Wellesley; the distance from my parents was awful. After hearing about my sorrows by phone, Dad sent me the collected works of Robert Frost along with a letter directing me to one poem in particular, "Reluctance." Dad's message and gift were meant to soothe me, and to say, through poetry, that all would be well.

> Ah, when to the heart of man
> Was it ever less than a treason
> To go with the drift of things,
> To yield with a grace to reason,
> And bow and accept the end
> Of a love or a season?[6]

---

6. Excerpt from Robert Frost's "Reluctance," *A Boy's Will* (London: David Nutt, 1913).

CHAPTER 2

ᗯᐯᐯᐸ

The Theoretical Physicist

Sid Drell was a theoretical physicist during a period when physicists were rocking the world with their great strides forward in the realms of physics, astronomy, energy, quantum mechanics, medicine, and many other fields.

But high schooler Sidney, for whom physics was the "worst course ever," could not have imagined such an exalted role in the field for himself. Young Drell did find some benefit, however, in applying mathematics to physics problems, which may have proved the spark to his eventual career.

As for his choice of university, "Nobody I knew had heard of Princeton, but I had heard of Einstein! It was Einstein's academic reputation that called to me. I was aware that he was somehow associated with Princeton, and it struck me that if I were admitted to the university where Einstein was, I would surely attend."

Drell applied and was accepted. When he shared the good news with his parents, his father's enthusiastic response was, "And I will pay your tuition!"

So off Drell went to Princeton at age sixteen, on top of the world. But by the end of his first week there, his father was hospitalized with a serious illness, thus negating the promise to finance his son's education.

"I will always remember how miserable he was when, at the end of my second week, I announced that I would work my way through school," Drell said. Princeton's administration was understanding, and offered a scholarship for tuition and job opportunities for work on campus to keep freshman Drell solvent. Some of the jobs involved parking cars at the football stadium before the games and waiting tables. "By my senior year," he boasted, "I was so good at the tasks that I became captain of the waiters! And, although these were jobs my father viewed as demeaning, I saw them as the practical way to get myself through school."

Drell was one of a very small number of incoming freshmen who had attended public school, but with ongoing interactions, especially among young students, any "us versus them" barriers tended to vanish. What's more, who could resist Drell's endearing personality or readily engaged intelligence? In this instance, the situation played out in ways that glass-half-full Drell found beneficial to both sides:

> Looking back, I realized that if I'd had any advance knowledge of the privileged backgrounds of most of my fellow classmates-to-be, I would have decided to forgo attendance at Princeton. I would have been too wary of encountering likely disadvantages because I wasn't from a distinguished family; I was Jewish—a minority there. But the prep school boys provided those of us who were less well-off with opportunities to earn money and to share knowledge as we tutored them and served them meals.

And, too, America's involvement in World War II changed Princeton profoundly. "Social and economic distinctions melted away, no longer relevant to any of us as we all sustained the loss of classmates in the war," Drell explained.

John Wheeler, a theoretical physicist who had been involved in the Manhattan Project and also had worked with Niels Bohr, returned to campus in Drell's senior year and became his senior thesis adviser. Drell's subject was "propagated action at a distance theory," a topic

Portrait of Sid as a graduating
Princeton Tiger, 1946.

both Wheeler and Richard Feynman were pursuing at the time. In hindsight, Drell recognized that Wheeler was crucially important to his training: "My thesis work on radiating electrons and Wheeler's influence were the forces that spurred me on to graduate school and to my ultimate choice of a career as a physicist."

Drell turned eighteen in September 1944, took his draft board physical, and returned to Princeton, having already completed six semesters. (A three-semester year was instituted in the accelerated wartime academic program.) But by the time his draft notice arrived in January 1945, Drell was lying in a hospital bed fighting for his life; his appendix had ruptured and peritonitis had set in.

Recovering Amid Victims of War

During his four months of recuperation at home in Atlantic City, Drell observed firsthand the human costs of war. Before the war, the

big hotels there had been repurposed as basic training sites for soldiers going abroad, but by the spring of 1945 the Boardwalk was full
of the returning wounded. Witnessing the transformation was a terrible sight for young Drell.

"As I limped along, the soldiers commonly mistook me for one of
their own. We'd get to talking, and they would reveal heartbreaking
details of their war experiences." Seeing the suffering caused by war
made a deep impression on Drell, one that would affect significant
career decisions later in life.

Drell returned to Princeton in July 1945, having missed a semester. He was sure that he'd be drafted when fully recovered but, as he
remembered precisely, "come the sixth of August 1945, everything
changed."

That afternoon, he headed down to the customary Princeton tea
for mathematicians and physicists. "As an undergraduate, it was a big
deal for me to be included, because usually only graduate students
and professors were invited. I was officially an interloper, but in physics there's no caste system."

At the tea, a very senior mathematics professor walked in and,
according to Drell, announced emphatically, "I hear they just dropped
an atomic bomb on Hiroshima. I hope they built a second one, put all
the scientists who built the first one on an island, and then dropped it
on them!" Drell recalled the stunned silence that followed the professor's pronouncement. Nine days later, after the atomic destruction of
Nagasaki, Japan surrendered. It was much later that Drell's personal
and informed reaction to the bombings registered: "I have since come
to the conclusion that any idea that we *wouldn't* have used the bomb
back then was crazy."

Drell went on to finish the semester and graduate in 1946. He
praised his education at Princeton as being "outstanding . . . partly
because it has no professional schools, offering instead a great
research faculty that is heavily focused on undergraduate teaching. In
addition, its tradition of requiring an independent honors thesis is
unique and provides significant benefit to the students."

Drell remained forever loyal to Princeton, but he also developed a strong allegiance to his next academic home, the University of Illinois at Urbana-Champaign, to the degree that he described his time there as "four of the greatest years of my life."

America was being remade—signs of change were everywhere. The GI Bill had brought the privilege of a college education to millions, and campuses were buzzing as never before. Drell remembered that "getting a bed to sleep in was the hardest part of student life." For over a year, he and his 299 classmates were assigned makeshift quarters in the men's old gym.

Drell had been drawn to the University of Illinois by the strong reputation of its theoretical physics program, and the young Sidney Dancoff, a brilliant theoretical physicist, became his doctoral thesis adviser. Dancoff was a student of J. Robert Oppenheimer (of Manhattan Project fame) who had come back from Metallurgical Laboratory work at the University of Chicago after the war. Drell was his first advisee.

"I got lots of attention," Drell recalled in a 1986 interview. "Dancoff was both patient and wise. It was just great luck to have him as an adviser. It was also a tragedy when, less than two years after I received my PhD, he died of cancer. The memory of that loss still pains me."

Much later, James "bj" Bjorken, a student of Drell's at Stanford who became one of his most trusted friends and colleagues, noted of this period, "Sid's contributions to physics began with his thesis work at the University of Illinois under the supervision of Sidney Dancoff. His subject was meson theory, a frontier topic at the time that played a pivotal role in establishing his career arc." (Mesons are subatomic particles consisting of a quark and an antiquark, with a lifespan of a few billionths of a second.)

Having received his PhD from the University of Illinois in 1949, Drell considered three career options. The first was postdoctoral work at Princeton's Institute for Advanced Study, where Oppenheimer was the director. A second possibility was a position as a junior fellow at Harvard, where Drell was in the final competition. But before the results

(L to R) Charles Slichter, John Blair, and Sidney Drell in 1949: three
University of Illinois grad students whose bond was lifelong thereafter.

were announced, he had decided to go west and become a physics
instructor at Stanford. A highlight of that period for Drell was the
arrival at Stanford of Wolfgang "Pief" Panofsky, who came to head
the high energy laboratory.

After two years at Stanford, Drell returned to the East Coast in
1952, this time to become a research associate working with Victor
"Viki" Weisskopf, head of MIT's major theory operation. Weisskopf's
other research associate that year was Amos de-Shalit, who became
one of Drell's fast friends. The two remained close over the years, and
Drell recalled his delight in visiting his colleague at the Weizmann
Institute in Israel, where de-Shalit had founded the department of
nuclear physics and ultimately become the institute's chief executive.

At MIT, Drell's regard for Weisskopf was doubly grounded: "Viki
was a brilliant physicist, but he was also a wonderful musician."
Weisskopf often jokingly claimed that he'd offered Drell the job

solely on the basis of a specific recommendation from Felix Bloch, a Nobel Prize laureate and Stanford physicist, who had advised, "Don't worry about Sid's physics. He's a good violinist!"

Born in Vienna and educated in Germany and Denmark, Weisskopf was a veteran of postdoctoral work with some of the true titans: Werner Heisenberg, Erwin Schrödinger, Wolfgang Pauli, and Niels Bohr. When he came to the United States, and to MIT's physics department, Weisskopf brought a great deal of history along with him. A group leader of the theoretical division of the Los Alamos Manhattan Project during World War II, he later became a fervent advocate for nuclear nonproliferation. Drell remembered him as "one of my great teachers."

To Stanford to Stay

By 1956, after spending four years at MIT and having secured a faculty position, Drell had a tough choice to make: Should he remain at MIT for the long haul or accept an invitation to return to Stanford?

Fred Terman, Stanford's provost, and David Packard, head of the Stanford Board of Trustees, convinced Drell that Stanford was the best option because it was well on its way toward becoming a great university. In Drell's opinion, the ideas being considered at Stanford, and especially the university's emphasis on physics, were very compelling. This focus was due, in part, to the brothers Russell and Sigurd Varian and their work at Stanford on klystron technology, which had helped the Allies win World War II. The klystron is a power source for microwave radiation such as radar (essential technology during the Battle of Britain) but also for the electromagnetic fields that accelerate electrons on their way down a linear accelerator.

Drell added, "An important factor in Stanford's future was the work of Pief Panofsky, whom I had gotten to know during my first two years there after he'd 'defected' from Berkeley." Panofsky, a German American physicist, had left the University of California–Berkeley because he opposed the loyalty oaths requiring UC faculty there (and all state employees) to disavow radical beliefs. "So, fortunately—and notwithstanding the competing invitations from universities all over the nation—Panofsky chose Stanford," said Drell, who noted that "Pief's decision to move from Berkeley to Stanford to lead the high energy laboratory created a real transformation, making Stanford modern, in my view. As much as I was drawn to Stanford, without Panofsky's presence there, I probably would have stayed at MIT."

Drell also could see that life in California was good. The lure of being able to live on the Stanford campus was strong, especially when compared to the difficult commute he endured daily when heading to Cambridge, made necessary because the Drells couldn't afford to live anywhere near MIT. At the time, their son, Daniel, was three years old, and daughter Persis was barely three months old, making the family's quality of life a crucial factor in Drell's ultimate decision. Wrestling with the choice was tough, as he recalled: "I had four great years on the faculty at MIT. In fact, after my third year, when Stanford invited me back to take a permanent position, it took me a year to make up my mind. But I saw the future with 'the Monster' and Panofsky, and thought, 'Stanford is a beautiful place and it's got a fantastic future. I'm going to join them both.'"

So it was that, in 1956, Drell left MIT and joined Panofsky at Stanford in work on the Monster, or Project M, which was destined to become the two-mile-long linear particle accelerator at the Stanford Linear Accelerator Center (renamed the SLAC National Accelerator Laboratory in 2008). At Stanford, they worked together as close colleagues—Panofsky as director of the High Energy Physics Laboratory (HEPL), Drell as a professor of physics.

Drell wasn't the only physicist from MIT to make the move to Stanford. Others were equally drawn by the groundbreaking experiments of Stanford physicists into electron scattering from nuclei. This research was directed by Nobel laureate Robert Hofstadter and made possible by Panofsky's leadership in creating the 550 MeV (million electron volt) linear accelerator laboratory at HEPL, which had been

founded at Stanford in 1951. The emigration from MIT included
Burt Richter, Fred Zachariasen, Al Odian, Henry Kendall, Charlie
Schwartz, and bj Bjorken. As Bjorken recalled:

At MIT, Sid and Burt Richter were, I believe, strongly influenced
by mentor and guru Viki Weisskopf. Viki was a pre–World War II
pioneer in quantum electrodynamics, aka QED. But, despite the
postwar progress made by Feynman, [Julian] Schwinger, and
[Sin-Itiro] Tomonaga, Viki remained deeply skeptical about the
validity of QED at short distances. This skepticism was shared by
Sid and Burt when they emigrated to Stanford in 1956. Sid created a theoretical structure for evaluating the sensitivity of a
given experiment to a QED breakdown at short distances, and
Burt set out to do the appropriate measurements. I was caught in
the middle. Half of my thesis, together with Sid and fellow graduate student Steve Frautschi, involved the tedious calculations
needed for Burt's experiment. This required a yearlong hand cal-
culation that was done in triplicate in order to weed out our many
algebraic mistakes.

Adding more details of those memorable early days, Bjorken
continued:

During those Stanford years, Sid carried out the aforementioned
work with Charlie Schwartz and Leonard Schiff on electron scattering from nuclei. In addition, Sid and Fred Zachariasen wrote a
very nice short book on the electromagnetic structure of the proton and neutron. In its day, the book was important in the field,
and it was significant in that it served as an anchor to Sid's scientific interests at that time.[1]

---

1. The book is Sidney D. Drell and Fredrik Zachariasen, *Electromagnetic Structure of Nucleons* (London and New York: Oxford University
Press, 1961).

From 1961 to 1962, Drell and his family took leave of Stanford to spend a year in Geneva, where he worked at CERN, the European Organization for Nuclear Research. A major goal for CERN in the 1950s was to create a unifying effect for research in fundamental physics and in the process foster peaceful cooperation among European nations that had recently been at war with one another. In the 1960s, CERN joined with the United States and the Soviet Union in providing a neutral ground for science during the height of the Cold War.

In a 1998 article for SLAC's *Beam Line*, Drell recalled, in more technical language, the unifying effect that CERN had on the physics community:

> With the creation of CERN in Geneva, we truly became one international community collaborating productively on experiments and theories. Parity fell, and we learned the beauty of broken symmetry, spontaneous and otherwise. Muons and neutrinos came into the fold and a theory of weak interactions was completed. We dispersed, analytically continued, and Reggeized to study strong interactions. The proton and neutron revealed their inner structures and acquired many relatives in a strange particle zoo with new symmetries and selection rules; eventually quantum chromodynamics or QCD—a non-abelian gauge theory of quarks and gluons, with confinement and asymptotic freedom—was developed as a fundamental field theory of the strong interactions.[2]

Drell was back at Stanford when construction began in 1962 on what would become the world's longest and straightest structure at the time. As recorded in a brief history in SLAC's strategic plan, published in November 2014:

---

2. Sidney D. Drell, "Reflections," *Beam Line* 28, no. 2 (Summer 1998), 5–6.

Project M would accelerate electrons to nearly the speed of light for groundbreaking experiments in creating, identifying and studying subatomic particles. Stanford University leased the land to the federal government for the new Stanford Linear Accelerator Center and provided the brainpower for the project, setting the stage for a productive and unique scientific partnership that continues today, made possible by the sustained support and oversight of the U.S. Department of Energy.[3]

Success at SLAC

With construction under way on the Stanford Linear Accelerator, Drell, Panofsky, and others left Stanford's physics department in 1963 to establish SLAC's new lab. Drell gathered members for the first theory group, which included H. Pierre Noyes, Yung-Su "Paul" Tsai, and Samuel Berman. Joining them soon thereafter were Bjorken, Stanley Brodsky, and Fred Gilman, mainstays of the group that interpreted the inelastic scattering experiments carried out by SLAC in the late 1960s.[4] In 1969, Drell became executive head of the theory group, a position he held until 1986. Drell was also appointed deputy director of SLAC in 1969 and served in that role until his retirement in 1998. Years later, Bjorken credited Drell for much of the success that SLAC enjoyed in its early days:

Soon after Sid moved over to Project M, he discovered the Drell Process. It opened up an entire field of experimental physics—not anticipated at the time of creation of Project M—that could be

3. "SLAC Strategic Plan," SLAC National Accelerator Laboratory (November 2014): 6, www6.slac.stanford.edu/files/Strategic_Plan_2014.pdf.

4. Robert Jaffe and Raymond Jeanloz, *Sidney D. Drell (1926–2016): Biographical Memoirs* (Washington, DC: National Academy of Sciences, 2018), 8, http://www.nasonline.org/publications/biographical-memoirs/memoir-pdfs/drell-sidney.pdf.

carried out at the new accelerator. Because of this Drell Process, a large bubble chamber group based at UC Berkeley, complete with bubble chamber, emigrated to the laboratory and greatly enriched the laboratory program.[5]

Right from the beginning, when SLAC was no more than Project M, housed in a warehouse on the Stanford campus, Sid left the more familiar and comfortable world of academe to join the adventure of creating a new laboratory. After the laboratory staff moved from the Project M warehouse on the Stanford campus to the SLAC site, Sid's focus moved from the front office into the theory group and its activities. Pierre Noyes was the formal head of the theory group, and he set its course in a very productive direction. But over the years, Sid took the forefront and really shaped the personality of the theory group. A major challenge he faced, as a theorist, was to create the kind of intellectual climate more typically found in university departments and in those days not commonly found within the country's accelerator laboratories.[6]

This change turned into an incredible success story. Quickly the theory group became very well known, not only for the variety of talent it attracted but especially for its unique personality.

Burt Richter, the late Nobel laureate and director of SLAC from 1984 to 1999, also praised Sid's role in the theory group:

Sid did something that I think is remarkable and very much in character. He started off as the head of the theory group at SLAC,

5. The bubble chamber, which led to a Nobel Prize in physics for inventor Donald Glaser, makes the trails of subatomic particles visible as microscopic bubbles.

6. Other accelerator labs at the time were Lawrence Berkeley in Berkeley, California; Brookhaven in Upton, New York; and Argonne in Lemont, Illinois.

not the deputy director. The SLAC theory group ended up as the place where a very large fraction of what I would call the heroes of theoretical physics over the next twenty years spent some time as postdocs. Sid ran a theory group that was, I would say, a magnet for the theory community. At the time, it was the world's leading laboratory in particle physics even though it was relatively small.

Bjorken further described the active intellectual environment with ample capacity for creativity fostered by Drell:

The quality and style of the SLAC theory group in the 1970s was very special. There was a high standard of excellence together with a warm ambience. Informality, especially in the seminars, was the norm. Sid would often ask a question that would elicit stifled groans of, "Oh, God, doesn't he know the answer to that?" Then, in the course of dialogue with the speaker, it would become clear that there was much more to Sid's question than met the ear at first hearing; it wasn't naïve at all! Such questions would draw people in, creating a setting that encouraged everyone in the audience to participate without worrying that a question might be too dumb to pose.

To this day, this personality persists at SLAC: uncompromisingly high standards, a good mix of applied and formal theory, a close interaction with the experimental community, a breadth of vision, an essential humanitarianism, and an informality and lack of pretension that keep the pursuit of physics something not only deeply satisfying but also just plain fun to do.

The Drell-Bjorken friendship and collaboration spanned decades, and bj became part of the extended Drell family. Reflecting on their relationship, Bjorken said, "Sid has been everything to me, as a teacher and mentor, as a second father, as an esteemed colleague, as best man at my wedding, and simply as a dear friend."

One of the SLAC Boys of
Summer, representing the
Theorists in battle against
the Experimentalists;
here in a seventh-inning
brewski break, 1982.

Fred Gilman, a member of the SLAC faculty from 1969 to 1990, remembered Sid's honesty, firm convictions, and leadership during those years: "Steady and caring, Sid would tell you what he thought. Evidence could change Sid's mind, but his core principles did not change and he would ardently defend them."

While Drell thrived at the highest levels of scientific research, he also took time for more lighthearted pursuits with his fellow physicists at SLAC. Haim Harari, Annenberg Professor of High Energy Physics at the Weizmann Institute of Science, where he was president from 1988 to 2001, spent two years at SLAC as a postdoctoral fellow. He recalled the occasion in 1970 when he, along with Gilman and another young SLAC professor, turned thirty:

> We bemoaned the fact that, unlike those in the pantheon of great physicists, we had not enjoyed important breakthroughs by this, our thirtieth year. Einstein's theory of relativity breakthrough was at age twenty-six, Heisenberg's quantum mechanics, along with other discoveries, at twenty-six. Almost never do breakthroughs happen to scientists after the age of thirty. Because of our shared misery, Sid invited the three families for a "wake" at his house, complete with a mock declaration of the end of our careers.

Drell and his colleague Richter also organized an annual softball game, with the theorists on one team and the experimental physicists opposing them. Drell's daughter Persis remembers it as "a golden era back then, including softball with doughnuts and beer. SLAC was the center of the universe for particle physics in those years. The theory group was famous, its culture and tone set by my father. There was no question that scientists thrived there."

Richard Blankenbecler, SLAC professor emeritus, was another one of Drell's graduate students in the late 1950s for whom Sid was a role model. He credits Drell as the exemplar who motivated his own decision to focus later in his career on ameliorating scientific technology's unintended impacts on mainstream society. Of Drell's important role as his thesis adviser, he said, "Sid was truly great with students—openhearted and inclusive." Harari, too, applauded Drell as "one of the best teachers and mentors to young aspiring scientists":

> Sid's perspective, which he put into practice throughout his long career, was that scientists owe it to their community, to their country, and to humanity to do their best to alleviate science-related problems. Sid maintained this conviction throughout his

life and spread his love of learning and love of life, along with his commonsensical approach to every endeavor, to all who were fortunate enough to encounter him. Like a bee, flower to flower, he has enriched every field he has pollinated.

It was during their early years at SLAC that Drell and Bjorken coauthored two important textbooks. For many years, their *Relativistic Quantum Mechanics* (1964) was considered the bible in its sphere. Their second book, *Relativistic Quantum Fields*, was published in 1965.[7]

Drell's areas of expertise were quantum electrodynamics, the study of the interactions between electromagnetic quanta (photons) and their charged-particle sources, and quantum chromodynamics, which describes the interaction between strong-interaction quanta (gluons) and their quark sources.

Drell had long been interested in the anomalous magnetic moment of the nucleon, and in the 1960s, there was a growing interest among physicists in studying how electromagnetic and weak interaction currents invited associations among processes that could be converted into sum rules. From 1962 through 1964, Drell worked with theoretical physicist Anthony Hearn, a research associate at Stanford, to formulate the Gerasimov-Drell-Hearn sum rule relating "the anomalous magnetic moment of any target to the difference of cross sections for absorption of photons of different polarizations."[8]

From 1968 to 1970, Drell worked closely with another SLAC research associate, Tung-Mow Yan. Now a professor emeritus at Cornell University, Yan recalled his tenure at SLAC: "During those years, SLAC was a very exciting place to be. Sid's leadership qualities made the group the best—not only in the country but also in the whole world. He treated everyone—including graduate students and

---

7. Both were published by McGraw-Hill, New York.
8. Jaffe and Jeanloz, *Sidney D. Drell*, 9.

postdocs—with respect. The group was open, interactive, and productive. We all worked very hard but enjoyed it. Sid was somehow able to provide an exciting environment in which everyone could thrive." Research by Drell and Yan resulted in a 1970 paper, "Massive Lepton-Pair Production in Hadron-Hadron Collisions at High Energies," which describes what has become known as the Drell-Yan process.

Bjorken explained, "The Naïve Drell-Yan Formula describes how quarks and antiquarks present in colliding proton and antiproton beams annihilate into dileptons. The formula is simple, but subtle. With the development of quantum chromodynamics, the simple result that Sid and his colleague Tung-Mow Yan achieved has been embellished—hence the aforementioned prefix. I especially like the irony therein, because the concept of a naïve Drell is downright unthinkable!"

Lance Dixon, a professor of particle physics and astrophysics at SLAC, recalled attending a seminar at the University of Oregon and seeing a diagram of the Drell-Yan process engraved on the floor of the physics department's lobby. "It was an indication of how important that process was."

Building on the work done by Drell and Yan, François Englert and Peter W. Higgs won a Nobel Prize in physics in 2013 for discovering the Higgs boson (sometimes referred to as the God particle).

Persis Drell remarked, "I don't think the Nobel was ever an interest for my father, though some of his work proved foundational to the efforts of other physicists who became Nobel laureates. The Drell-Yan process is the basis for what was used at CERN, the European Organization for Nuclear Research in Geneva, to discover the Higgs."

Bureaucratic Turf Wars

Notwithstanding great successes and despite major contributions to humankind, even science must reckon with bureaucracy. "In the early

1960s," Drell recalled, "the physics department balked at allowing SLAC to have any faculty. We fought hard, with [then] provost Fred Terman's support, maintaining that if we were to attract good, qualified people, we had to be able to offer professorships to them."

When Terman made the decision to create a new, separate faculty for SLAC, the physics department relented, allowing SLAC to have professors, but no graduate students. Drell's immediate response was, "How can I offer a professorship to a colleague without any students to teach? If that condition is enforced, I quit." So that's just what he did, leaving the physics department in 1963 to become a professor at SLAC along with Panofsky, SLAC's first director.

In the end, the administration did come around, just as Drell had anticipated. SLAC's success was due, indeed, to its ability to attract the best people from the best universities, confer professorships, and allow them to have graduate students.

But that was not to be the last clash with the physics department. Drell described how, during SLAC's early years, the department became concerned that the allocation of funds to hire high energy physicists at SLAC would limit the number of appointments that could be made in other areas of physics at Stanford. The department contended that it should never have fewer professors than SLAC had:

> In other words, SLAC's rate of growth would be restricted by a balancing provision controlled by the physics department. I protested that such a policy would restrict SLAC's growth, but Dick Lyman, president of Stanford, was adamantly against our rationale and sent Bill Miller, his provost, to tell me so. I responded, "Thank you, Bill. Go back to campus and tell Dick Lyman that I quit." I had just received a major offer from MIT. "Wait a minute," Bill said. He picked up the phone, called Lyman, and they folded.

Richter recalled another dynamic perspective on the controversy: "Here was the largest facility in the world at the time. SLAC was the

Drell and John Lewis, director of Stanford's Arms Control and Disarmament Program, present a "beam tree"—electron beams captured in plastic at almost the speed of light—to Geng Biao, China's vice premier and minister of defense, in Beijing, 1981.

first $100 million construction for science—and they [the physics department] didn't want to let anybody at it. It was a very interesting battle."

Drell recounted more about this period with great clarity:

During the six months that the great Panofsky took a sabbatical, I was acting director of SLAC. I did a good job, including negotiating with the director of the Lawrence Berkeley Laboratory to build the Positron-Electron Project (PEP) collider as a joint effort. Even so, I disliked the responsibilities within the role of director because I had no opportunity to sit quietly and focus on whatever I wanted to think about. So I kept handy, in my top desk drawer, a letter of resignation, complete except for the date, which I left blank. It was a "just in case" letter, ready if circumstances dictated my need to tender it, because I didn't want to miss a beat when the time came.

I didn't have a particular image of the event that would trigger that decision, but I had no doubt that I would know it when I encountered it because it would involve a matter for serious managerial intervention. And, as just about everyone who knows me well is aware, I am not the managerial type. I have no desire to run things. I was never permanent director of SLAC, and I had never opted to accept any official position I was offered in Washington, simply because I knew my limitations.

Drell's determined adherence to his principles, evidenced throughout his career, was in full view during another controversy that arose in the late 1980s. Political scientist John Lewis and Drell were cofounders and codirectors from 1983 to 1989 of Stanford's Center for International Security and Arms Control (CISAC, now the Center for International Security and Cooperation). Drell had emphasized to Donald Kennedy, Stanford's president at the time, that it was essential for CISAC to have the power to confer professorships.

He recalled, "Candidates of the caliber we needed would expect benefits commensurate with their expertise. In our negotiations with the administration, we even gave up the possibility of tenure." (Just as Drell learned that he had tenure—a fact revealed in the course of his negotiations—he would give it up with this bargain.)

Don was not opposed to our proposal, but his provost, Jim Rosse, was firmly against it. I reminded them that we'd had this fight before in our effort to make professorships available to SLAC scientists. We had won and gone on to build a great machine— the most successful one in the world. Rosse's rejoinder was, "Well, physics is physics, but you can't make professorships out of a field that may go away." I was astonished to hear him call arms control "a field that may go away."

The university also wanted CISAC to be funded by contract money. Even though we offered to raise the money ourselves, they refused. They added that if the program should run out of funds—which would not have happened—at least there would be no university tenure to protect.

Sadly, we lost Sally Ride, an eminent physicist who had joined us after her retirement from NASA. She had made significant contributions during her two years with us. When the decision was made to deny her tenured professor status at CISAC, however, she left for a more unrestrained opportunity at UC San Diego, and then went on to create a private program for women pursuing careers in science. [Ride, a Stanford alumna, was also the first American woman in space.]

Thereafter unable to gain the right to confer permanent professorships on several outstanding scholars at CISAC, Drell resigned in November 1988.

From Physics to Public Policy

Gradually, as chapter 3 illustrates, Drell's influence extended far beyond particle physics as he was drawn into the public-policy issues of strategic defense and arms control in the early 1960s. Bjorken described Drell's role as exemplifying for everyone the value and need of public service: "One small expression of his influence is that some of his students and other physicists passing through the SLAC environment have chosen to move their careers out of physics and into public affairs. Quite a few others, while staying within physics, have been especially active in the social issues created by the big-science character of particle physics."

Drell's commitment to public-policy issues also led him to foster and encourage the development of the Stanford Workshops on Political and Social Issues (SWOPSI). Bob Jaffe, Joyce Kobayashi, and Joel

Trailblazers in Project M's initial brain trust gathered for SLAC's twentieth anniversary, 1982: (L to R) engineer Ed Ginzton and physicists Sid Drell, bj Bjorken, Burt Richter, and Pief Panofsky.

Primack, all Stanford students when they met Drell, organized the workshops in 1969 and agreed that, as Kobayashi put it, "Sid was our center of gravity" in this ambitious endeavor. She recalled Sid's "loyal relationships and the goals he pursued, grounded in deeply held beliefs that defined a life of ethical significance. The lifelong commitment of individuals like Sid Drell presents us with a call to conscience. . . . I believe his most important accomplishment may be that legacy."

Jaffe, now a professor of physics at MIT, said, "I think Sid's model of constructive interaction between scientists and government was . . . a core idea in formulating the program. It was a very compelling image to students like us." Primack, now a professor of physics and astrophysics at the University of California–Santa Cruz, recalled Sid's influence: "What remains is the lasting inspiration Sid provided to tackle things outside my scientific work and to attempt to improve the way our government and our society deal with science and technology issues." Notable here is the fact that both Jaffe and Primack went on to broaden their physics careers, Jaffe in science and technology policy, and Primack in educating the public in the field of cosmology. Primack, like Drell, was also awarded the Leo Szilard Lectureship Award for "outstanding accomplishments by physicists in promoting the use of physics for the benefit of society."

Meanwhile, at SLAC, Drell's legacy lives on. The brain trust responsible for SLAC's development and extraordinary success spans from Panofsky and Drell himself to Richter and Jonathan Dorfan, and down to another Drell—Persis, director from 2007 through October 2012—to the current helmsman, Chi-Chang Kao.

Among the multitude of projects SLAC scientists have contributed to and participated in are the Large Hadron Collider and its ATLAS experiment and science program at CERN; the Enriched Xenon Observatory in New Mexico; the Fermi Gamma-ray Space Telescope; research at the Kavli Institute for Particle Astrophysics and Cosmology; the Large Synoptic Survey Telescope (the world's largest camera); the Stanford PULSE Institute; the Stanford Synchrotron Radiation Lightsource; and the Super Cryogenic Dark Matter Search experiment.

From 1962, when construction of the Monster began, to the present, SLAC has expanded its mission and influence. Its success has powerfully validated Drell's instinct, which propelled him from MIT to a permanent home in California, that Stanford and SLAC were in the vanguard of a brilliant future—a future facilitated by and, in tandem with other trailblazers, brought to fruition by Drell himself.

CHAPTER 3

∿

In Service to Country: Jason and the Cold War

Sid Drell was a man fully engaged in many arenas, choosing to immerse himself in worthy pursuits with great enthusiasm and devotion. It was his nature to find meaning in wide-ranging issues and to contribute where his abilities might prove helpful and when he was called upon to serve. In the realm of politics and government, Drell traced the impetus for his many years of advising the federal government back to American scientist Vannevar Bush's 1945 report to President Truman. *Science, the Endless Frontier* laid out a visionary blueprint for the postwar support of science and pressed for expansion of government funding. During World War II, Bush was director of the Office of Scientific Research and Development, responsible for all wartime R&D, including the Manhattan Project. He also championed a movement that led to the founding of the National Science Foundation.

Drell wrote about Bush and his influence in an article for SLAC's *Beam Line* publication: "[Bush] reminded Washington [DC] that research is a difficult and often very slow voyage over uncharted seas and therefore, for science to flourish with governmental support, freedom of inquiry must be preserved, and there must be funding stability over a period of years so that long-range programs may be undertaken and pursued effectively."[1]

With his sharp sense of history, Drell was inspired as he witnessed the great heroes of modern science offering their expertise in government service. "These people were my role models—and what role models they were! They included I. I. Rabi, Robert Oppenheimer, Pief Panofsky, and Hans Bethe, among others." (These scientists all were active in public-policy debates as well as nuclear physics.) "They modeled a principled response to the need for scientists to accept responsibility for the moral questions posed when their scientific findings evolved to suggest applications."

From their example, Drell understood that the impact of science created a moral obligation: "It is incumbent upon the community of scientists—who are the most competent and informed, having discovered and generated new forms of knowledge—to disclose to leaders in government any inherent drawbacks, any possible effects or social implications there might be."

And then came Jason.

Drell explained the backdrop: "As Washington was grappling with ways to address the urgency of these realities, Jason was born, its mission to gather a small group of young scientists willing to work on problems or issues that were consequential to scientific developments. There were thirty to thirty-five recruits identified; I was one of them. Charlie Townes, a physicist informally known as the father of Jason, called one night to invite me to join the group."

Purportedly named for the Greek mythological figure who led the Argonauts in search of the Golden Fleece, Jason began as a consortium of physicists, all of whom were associated with government consulting. The group came together in 1960 and established an independent summer research program to study science and technology issues related to US national security. Drell recalled:

---

1. Drell, "Reflections," 4.

First of all, one is honored to receive a phone call from Charlie. Then, knowing what we scientists did about the devastating potential of an atom bomb and its consequences—ten kilotons increased to megatons is exponentially horrifying—and having the inspiring examples set by my most immediate role models, Pief Panofsky and Hans Bethe, as they answered the call to duty in advising government, how could I justify escaping the duty myself? I could not isolate myself from the world when that kind of responsibility called to me.

With ample justification, Drell felt the opportunity to join Jason as a founding member in 1960 was exactly right for him. It was a chance to be of service by solving problems with physics and advising the government on how the fruits of science could be used. He didn't want a job in Washington, as he said, "because of my aversion to what a commitment of that sort would mean," mainly in terms of the effects it would have on his family. Then again, even though joining Jason meant "I would be sacrificing my summers, which could have been given over to industrial consulting that paid well . . . working with the Jason group fit neatly within my priorities and had the additional benefit of satisfying my interest in being of service to my country." Reflecting on the effects of past experiences, Drell recognized why an affiliation with Jason held such appeal for him:

In a major way, I can say that the genesis of my interest in matters of war and peace is connected to the exceptional good fortune I had in escaping the war. Being sidelined with a life-threatening illness, I was unable to heed the draft's call, thereby missing an opportunity to exercise what I considered a duty of honor. And, as I recuperated at home, I became acquainted with some of the returning wounded soldiers and learned about the brutalities of war I'd been spared. Those encounters stuck with me along with the disproportional luck that fate had allowed, leaving me with the need to contribute somehow, some way.

Subconsciously, I had counted on having the chance to repay the
debt I felt I owed, and here was Jason, the place and opportunity
where I could do just that.

During the first summer session of Jason, Drell worked on a problem concerning missile launching and the ability to detect such
launches (a project called the Defender). "Once I'd had success with
that effort, I was certain that I'd made the right choice to become a
Jason. I was sold on it by the dual purposes to be served: I could do
scientific work and also advise about the possible policy implications
of that work."

An Outsider's Insider

President Eisenhower recognized the validity of Drell's determination
to remain an "outsider's insider" in Washington, DC, telling Edwin
Land, project director of the intelligence group that advised on the
U-2 reconnaissance program, "Oh, I'm so grateful to you fellows
who are from out of town. You can't think in Washington. You go
away and think and then you tell me what you've been thinking.
There's no way to think if you live here."[2] Eisenhower offered further
expression of admiration for citizen-scientists when he characterized
them to Jim Killian, who had chaired the President's Foreign Intelligence Advisory Board: "This bunch of scientists was one of the few
groups . . . I encountered in Washington who seemed to be there to
help the country and not help themselves."[3]

The Jasons aimed to balance science with public policy and were
particularly vocal about nuclear security. As Ann Finkbeiner writes in
The Jasons: The Secret History of Science's Postwar Elite, "The clus-
ter within Jason that deals with this genie is the arms controllers.
Though younger Jasons joined the arms controllers, its core was the

---

2. Philip Taubman, *Secret Empire: Eisenhower, the CIA, and the Hidden
Story of America's Space Espionage* (New York: Simon & Schuster, 2003), 90.

3. Taubman, 90.

older Jasons, including Drell, Garwin, and Dyson."[4] (Richard Garwin designed the first hydrogen bomb; Freeman Dyson was connected to Project Orion, which proposed space flight using nuclear pulse propulsion.) Finkbeiner quotes William Happer, a fellow Jason (a pioneer of adaptive optics who had joined in 1976): "I think particularly of Sid Drell, his whole life has been to try to put the genie back in the bottle."[5]

Drell and his cohort were part of a larger movement of scientists concerned with nuclear security. Physicist Bill Press said of this contingent: "[They] are actually the local chapter of a national group— not just a clique within Jason, but a whole generation of scientists. They're the scientists who are going to keep nuclear weapons under control even if they have to do it with their bare hands."[6]

Drell had been working with Jason for two years when, in 1962, he received a Saturday afternoon phone call from Albert "Bud" Wheelon, the CIA's first deputy director in charge of space and technology (he had helped develop America's first intercontinental ballistic missile [ICBM]). Drell recalled details of their acquaintance: "I met Bud at MIT when I arrived there after my two years as an instructor at Stanford. Bud was finishing up his thesis, and we became friends. He was a brilliant guy—he would later receive the US Distinguished Intelligence Medal—and he was very gentlemanly for a person as accomplished as he was in science."

In his capacity at the CIA, and with the circumspection one might expect, Wheelon addressed the purpose of the phone call: "Sid, I've got a problem. Could you get yourself to Washington tomorrow?" Of course he could, and he did.

Wheelon gave directions to the Key Bridge Marriott and an address on Washington Parkway. "All the cabbies know it," he promised. The next day, Drell arrived at the appointed place in Washington and was

---

4. Ann Finkbeiner, *The Jasons: The Secret History of Science's Postwar Elite* (New York: Penguin, 2006), 181.
5. Finkbeiner, *Jasons*, 181.
6. Finkbeiner, *Jasons*, 181.

President Johnson (right), with chemist Donald Hornig (center), welcomes
Drell to membership on the President's Science Advisory Committee, 1966.

immediately given clearances provided only to people who were
working in very-limited-access areas. The project he had been assigned
concerned the technical possibilities of gaining intelligence from
space-based satellite systems as a way of piercing the Iron Curtain
erected by the Soviet government. This was Corona.

The US-USSR "missile gap," as it was imagined to exist in the
1950s and early 1960s, was a major national security issue for the
United States. The launchings of *Sputnik* 1 and 2, along with major
crises involving aggressive activities by the Soviet Union, were also in
the background, creating tensions in Washington about means of
gathering intelligence to assess the actual capabilities of the Soviet
Union. With new "eyes in the skies"—the development of the U-2
reconnaissance aircraft—the United States had gleaned some information about Soviet missile capabilities. But that ended when Francis
Gary Powers was shot down and taken prisoner in 1960 as he flew a
U-2 mission across the Soviet Union. With so much at stake, the Air
Force and the CIA jointly developed the Corona satellite system.

Drell wrote about the Corona project in SLAC's *Beam Line*:

Photoreconnaissance from satellites circling the earth above the atmosphere at altitudes above a hundred miles enabled the US to pierce the shroud of secrecy by means that were effective, and that were accepted as non-provocative. With the photography brought back to earth we could more accurately assess the growing threat of Soviet nuclear warheads mounted on intercontinental range missiles and bombers. Subsequently it also opened the path to arms control. Since we could count and size the Soviets' threatening strategic forces from the satellite photographs, we could negotiate treaties and verify compliance with treaty provisions to limit their deployment and to initiate reductions. Photoreconnaissance satellites were the first big step toward achieving the Open Skies that President Eisenhower had first called for in 1955.[7] [Eisenhower had suggested that the Soviets and the Americans provide each other with maps of their military facilities so that each side could conduct aerial surveillance of the other to ensure arms control compliance. The Soviets rejected the idea.]

In conversation later, Drell recalled the project's history:

The decision to proceed with the Corona project was made in a special briefing session with Henry Kissinger [at that time a national security consultant] that Dick Garwin and I put together with people involved in the CIA. We convinced them that we should take advantage of the fact that the technology was beginning already in the civilian sector. Many years later [in July 2016], when Henry and I had a conversation about that pivotal meeting,

7. Drell, "Reflections," 8–9.

I said, in a little good-natured raillery, "Well, Henry, you know, we approved of at least one thing you did!"

At the beginning of the project, John Wheeler informed me, "I've got the engineers who have built this machine; different parts of it are from different companies. I need somebody I can trust to head this study and get me answers to problems with those parts." So I requested that my panel work with information and knowledge from the engineers and technical people in all of the industries responsible for making the Corona.

This added responsibility meant that, during this period, Drell's time would be divided among three professional duties: academic research, teaching, and government work on national security issues. He described his weekly agenda, set to accommodate extensive travel in the mix: "For those months, I arrived home on Thursday night, gave lectures on Friday, and then made time to spend with the family before returning to Washington on Monday."

As for his Jason assignment, Drell offered details:

The problem with the satellite's photographs took three to four months to solve. We discovered that when the very thin film was running extremely fast, an electrical charge would build up, causing white streaks that rendered some parts of the film unreadable. With the problem solved, I was responsible for briefing the director of the CIA and Edwin Land, inventor of instant photography and head of Polaroid-Land, the company manufacturing the reconnaissance satellites. At the time, Land was also an adviser to the president and an advocate for the building and increased usage of such satellites.

At the beginning, I had no idea what I was getting myself into, but this project brought me into a leadership role—and more. Along with Mal Ruderman, my colleague and collaborator on the project and a scientist I place in the league of a Gauss [German mathematician and physicist Johann Carl Friedrich Gauss (1777–1855)], we accomplished something useful. At its conclusion, I felt as though I'd offered a service to my country. However, I couldn't have anticipated the long-term implications of our achievement.

According to Drell, the result of the Corona project was an "awareness that we were ushering in a new era of information gathering and helping to provide a clear understanding of the Soviets' military capacities. We would learn that those powers had been overestimated, giving rise to the faulty assessment that had affected us profoundly."

Garwin, who later served with Drell on the Land Panel (named for Edwin Land), characterized the Corona project as a "highly secret field" and praised the work: "The amazing rate of progress in satellite reconnaissance capabilities during the Corona era was due in large part to the openness within this tightly secured community." Impressed by Drell's work on the project, Bud Wheelon said, "It was a heck of a job. . . . You just have to be very methodical, very penetrating, very patient, and very organized. And Sid's a very good guy to do that." As for Drell's management style, Wheelon remarked, "He led not by domination."[8]

With the completion of the Corona project, Drell was on his way to a career in government advising as an outsider's insider—or vice versa. He said of it, "Once I got so deeply involved in Jason work, particularly in solving the Corona problem, there was no way I was going to leave."

A Medal and a Milestone

As a result of the Corona project's success, the National Reconnaissance Office, an agency of the US Department of Defense, acknowledged, in 2000, Drell and his teammates as the original ten "Founders of National Reconnaissance." Drell, along with Senator Warren Rudman, a Republican from New Hampshire, received the highest

8. Albert "Bud" Wheelon, quoted in Philip Taubman, *The Partnership* (New York: HarperCollins, 2012), 111.

award given to civilians for contributions to the US intelligence community, the National Intelligence Distinguished Service Medal, in 2001.

Speaking in 2016, Drell said, "Of my awards, the National Intelligence Distinguished Service Medal means the most to me because the work we accomplished had a direct and immediate impact. The whole principle of my life in academia is that the more I, or a student, understand something, the wiser the decisions will be. Information is very important. We had the missile gap all wrong until we saw the evidence. The Corona satellite provided so much more coverage than could have been derived from the U-2."

The nuclear age thrust scientists—especially physicists—into the political world and the national conversation as never before. Drell's willingness to lend his scientific prowess to the government, combined with his diplomatic talents and his ability to work with people from many backgrounds, led to ever-increasing claims on his time. Although he took great satisfaction in government service, Drell's membership in various advisory groups, especially Jason, resulted in some contentious situations.

During his years at SLAC, Drell occasionally lectured in Europe, where he had some unsettling encounters in the early 1970s. When reports on Jason and the names of some of its members were publicly released through the leaking of the classified Vietnam War history known as the Pentagon Papers, the information provided fuel for the fires of anti–Vietnam War protests. Jason members were pilloried for aiding the US government in the war. Drell's identity as a Jason had been exposed through the theft of another Jason member's files. In fact, Drell had never been part of a Jason team that worked on Vietnam War–related issues—his attention in Jason being devoted exclusively to matters concerning the ballistic missile system.

Drell recognized and regretted the unintended consequences that came with some of Jason's interventions and political advising activities:

Many people who got involved in the [Vietnam War's McNamara Line] electronic barrier went in with the best of motives and saw some of the technical contributions they made used in ways that they feel quite unhappy about. But that's inevitable, you know. The laws of physics are fixed. The laws of politics change. And you're supping with the Devil in a difficult way. It's to be expected. It's unavoidable. And you have to keep your guard up.[9]

Perhaps that was a reason for opining, "I'd rather be working on particle physics problems. But if I can find a technical problem where I think the policy implications for national security are important, to me that's Jason work."[10]

While on sabbatical as a visiting professor at the University of Rome in the spring of 1972, Drell was invited to speak on the scientific work he had been engaged in there. When he arrived at the auditorium to give his lecture, he encountered an angry group of protesters. Drell recalled the setting:

Graduate students, fellows, and faculty members were in the audience. As I began to speak, one of the postdocs stood up and interrupted, saying, "Professor Drell, we know that you are a member of Jason, doing terrible things in Vietnam. We want your analysis of the United States' Vietnam policy, and then we'll vote on whether you can speak about your current scientific work here." I responded by cautioning the audience about the type of behavior they were exhibiting. I told them plainly, "This is fascism, and I will not submit to it or to an inquisition in order to give a science lecture. Furthermore, I'll be glad to discuss the issues you mention after my lecture. I've been here all spring and have been available during that time. And now, I'm also

9. Drell, quoted in Finkbeiner, *Jasons*, 93.
10. Drell, quoted in Finkbeiner, *Jasons*, 180.

available and willing to answer your questions, but not as a condition to giving my lecture." There was a lot of shouting back and forth, and then they left. No sooner had I resumed speaking than the few-in-number but disruptive students returned—accompanied by a crowd of people they had recruited from the plaza outside.

One of my graduate students intervened and arranged a meeting with the disrupters. We tried to talk with them, but our efforts were to no avail. I picked up my papers and headed for the only exit, which was in the back of the auditorium, where the protesters were gathered. They didn't touch me as I made my way through the swarm, but, frustrated by my lack of reaction, the hecklers resorted to yelling "Fire!" Then, of course, the entire building had to be cleared. The next day, I was followed around the campus and peppered with insults in Italian.

Within two weeks of my experience in Rome, I was in Erice, Sicily, to give a summer school lecture. The minute I began to speak, the Jason issue came up, but this time, the head of the school was completely prepared. He was in contact with the gendarmes, who tossed out the protesters, and I went ahead with my lecture.

Still, the protests continued unabated. Drell recalled the incident that followed as a mixed blessing of sorts:

By the time we arrived in Corsica for another summer school series of lectures, the Rome controversy had made the newspapers throughout Europe. Consequently, the minute I opened my mouth to speak, students began to protest, demanding, "You must first tell us about your involvement with Jason and Vietnam."

I refused to capitulate on two grounds: first, it was none of their business; and second, I was in no way related to the work they were accusing me of.

Attempting to quell tempers, the administration gave the pro-
testing students twenty-four hours to resolve the issue, allowing
that I would first give the lecture and then answer their questions
and concerns. The protesters refused to comply, so the administration closed the school. Perhaps as poetic justice, Harriet,
Persis, and I spent the unexpected free time swimming and relax-
ing at a resort on that beautiful island.

Ideological ugliness didn't come only from students. When Drell
was scheduled to speak at CERN, the European Organization for
Nuclear Research in Geneva, the directors were prepared, warned as
they had been by the extensive newspaper coverage of the protests at
his previous talks. The directors had organized a pre-lecture meeting,
and the auditorium was packed for the occasion.

"In attendance were several other physicists who, disappointingly,
offered only qualified support for my position," Drell recalled. "There
were even some respectable scientists in the audience who verbally
attacked me, but I stood firm. My daughter Persis was in the auditorium, and she remembers her shock on hearing one of the scientists
call me a prostitute for the Jason work he presumed I was doing."

While Drell expected that Jason would soak up a good deal of his
time and energy, he may not have anticipated the effect it would have
on his family. Persis did indeed remember that and other incidents in
Europe:

It was 1972, a time of much unrest. The invasion of Cambodia
was under way. The list of Jasons was circulating in Europe,
making my father persona non grata. He was thrown out of a
classroom in Rome, and a school in Corsica was closed down
because of his presence. The students were insisting that my
father talk first about his political views before giving his lectures, but he refused on principled grounds. He offered to discuss politics with the students, but not as a prerequisite to the
scheduled physics lectures. They just couldn't come to an

agreement, so the school was closed down. My father was crystal-clear about his reasons for working with the government. I sat in the audience and listened as my father was called a prostitute.

In the end, my father's strategy to work as a technical, non-political expert on issues of arms control and disarmament led to his tremendous influence over decades. His fingerprints are on all the major arms control treaties, legislations, and policies over fifty years because that's the way he, as an insider to the system, was determined to make an impact.

Scientist, Citizen, Bon Vivant

With the success of the Corona project, Drell was called repeatedly to serve on various other advisory groups to the federal government, including the President's Science Advisory Committee (PSAC) and its Ground Warfare Panel and Strategic Military Panel; the Land Panel, which focused on overhead reconnaissance; the High Energy Physics Advisory Board; and the President's Foreign Intelligence Advisory Board, much of whose work was, and remains, secret.

Drell's participation in PSAC presented an opportunity for informality and spontaneity that was rare in the usual settings of momentous responsibility. While serving on PSAC's Ground Warfare Panel, he was delighted to cast his vote for a bit of fun:

On one occasion, our group visited the combat development experimentation command at Fort Hunter Liggett, south of Monterey [California], where they were experimenting with new weapons and new forms of organization for small-unit combat. As we watched the demonstrations from the sidelines, one of our hosts said, "You guys are all working very hard. What would you like to do?" My immediate answer was, "Drive a tank!" My ensuing induction as an Honorary Tanker of the US Army provided a few moments of frivolity in otherwise serious business.

The late physicist Charles Slichter, one of Drell's PSAC colleagues and a longtime close friend from his University of Illinois days, described Drell's thoughtful consideration for others at that time:

Sid was chairman of a panel concerned with ground warfare, and I was a member of that panel. As the committee met once a month as a whole group and then in panels, we were able to see each other frequently.

The chairman of the President's Science Advisory Committee was Don Hornig, a famous chemist who later became president of Brown University. Hornig was terrible at keeping meetings on schedule, and this affected the many people who would come over from the Pentagon to give briefings on various scientific topics. As meetings were running late, these guests would sit and wait. By contrast, Sid, as chairman of the Ground Warfare Panel, made certain that we kept on schedule. He was conscious of the impact this had on our invited guests, over whom he had no authority but for whom he felt a duty to maintain timeliness. These guests recognized the importance of the panel's invitation and the opportunity to give a good account of themselves, so detaining them was unprofessional and inexcusable in Sid's mind. As a result, he made changes that emphasized the courtesy and respect such relationships and collaborations deserve.

The Ground Warfare Panel went on various field trips and, as its chairman, Sid would meet with the commanding officers of the groups we visited. It was wonderful to see how gracious he was, with that giant, warm smile and superb sense of humor.

Garwin was also a member of PSAC and, like Drell, was awarded the National Medal of Science. He has been described as "a true polymath . . . [who] has affected everyone's life with his more than benign inventions, from air traffic control systems to the first laser printer, and the touch-screen. . . . But, of the bomb, he once said, 'If I had a magic wand, I would make it go away' . . . [and he] has dedicated his life to producing that wand."[11] Garwin, whose high regard for Drell is obvious, said, "It has been my great pleasure to have been involved with Sid Drell in several activities through which he has performed such outstanding service toward US national security and the security of the world." He recalled times with Sid that merited his admiration:

> My first record of communication to Sid is a 1966 letter about PSAC membership. I had met him much earlier, when, applying knowledge I'd gleaned in my work with the PSAC Strategic Military Panel, I briefed the nascent Jason group on ballistic missile defense to share with them my thoughts and understanding of the technology and means of countering it. I worked very closely with Sid on PSAC panels and when we were both members of the Land Panel reporting on overhead reconnaissance. We had many other interactions, such as our campaign (beyond Washington) for rationality in regard to MX missile basing, where we had independent speaking tours of the Western states being considered as deployment areas for some of the basing modes. Once I became a Jason member myself, in 1966, my wife and I would spend time at the Jason Summer Study in La Jolla, where we were best friends (or so I like to think) with Sid and Harriet.
>
> Certainly, passion was a defining element of Sid's character, but so were integrity, caution, and perseverance. One of the reasons he was so effective is that he was a people person as well as a scientist and dedicated citizen.

Reflecting on joint efforts on the Land Panel, Garwin offered some memories:

---

11. Joel N. Shurkin, *True Genius: The Life and Work of Richard Garwin, the Most Influential Scientist You've Never Heard Of* (New York: Prometheus Books, 2017), ii.

Sid and I played a special role in getting approval from the Nixon administration, via Henry Kissinger, of the near-real-time digital imaging satellites, now ubiquitous. These satellites replaced the Corona system that operated from 1960 through 1972 and its successors, Gambit and Hexagon, all of which provided images from space by returning film to earth in protective reentry vehicles.

This was a high-tension activity, opposed by much of the bureaucracy; it succeeded only through my handwritten note to Henry Kissinger, delivered to him by an aide at a top-secret, special-access meeting, as I waited in the White House for a response. This activity was part of the reason that Sid and I were named, in 2000, by the National Reconnaissance Office, as two of the ten Founders of National Reconnaissance, along with Edwin Land and Bill Perry. Of course, for a very long time we couldn't talk about this, even to many of our friends with top-secret clearances, unless they had approved access to information about such space systems and a "need to know."

Noteworthy here are two influences that are the sine qua non of scientific inquiry, both underlying the experiences and the successes achieved in many of these endeavors. The first is reliance on strict adherence to the principles of the scientific method; the second is the model of operation and general ethos of the Jasons, grounded in the precepts of the scientific method by dint of the scientifically trained members and their purpose. These methodologies relied on synergism to guide the collective to cohesive wholeness and, as a result, onward to extraordinary results; and both were ground-setting approaches for Sid and his colleagues to rely upon in later years of collaborative work. For Sid, these approaches and the ambience they facilitated were complementary to his personality and character, as they were to many of his colleagues.

Drell's combination of scientific expertise, diplomacy, and devotion to country made him indispensable in Washington, DC, and

Sid, with other members of the Ground Warfare Panel, c. 1967: After arduous daylong exercises, Drell's chosen reward? *Driving a tank, of course!*

membership in Jason and other advisory groups resulted in strong personal and professional relationships. Longtime national security expert Mark Moynihan and Drell became close friends during their Jason summer sessions in La Jolla. He recalled:

> Every year, Sid and Harriet spent the summer in La Jolla so that Sid could attend the Jason Summer Study. They resided there in a high-security penthouse condominium, gated and closely watched by residents, so that a visitor had to be announced before being granted entry.
>
> On my first visit there, I went directly up to the Drells' apartment (not passing "Go," as they say) and knocked on their door,

unannounced. Sid opened the door, flabbergasted: "How did you get past security?" It was great fun to reply, "You forget, Sid, that I work for the CIA." Every year after that, I made it a point to get around any "high security" building and just show up at their door. Sid and Harriet found it highly amusing.

Drell's long friendship with physicist Bob Peurifoy, who worked at Sandia National Laboratories, also began with Jason efforts. Peurifoy contributed the following statement about his colleague:

Sid lives by his honor in doing what is right for the country. On several occasions, he has worked with me on national security issues, and I've never found any reason to question his expertise, his enthusiasm, or his willingness to put the country first. Those qualities are rare; I don't find them often anymore, unfortunately. Sid gets irritated, as we all do on occasion, with security problems, but he maintains a positive point of view. I can't say that about many people I know, so I consider him a bellwether.

The Citizen-Scientist

Near the end of his life, Drell himself recognized the importance of his efforts toward nonproliferation and commented on the impact of his choice to join Jason and participate in public service. In hindsight, he commented on the gratification he felt at having chosen to take on that role:

Within these past years, we've managed severe crises through these efforts in government advising. Collectively, we've avoided the use of nuclear weapons thus far; that's been enough to convince me that in my decisions to advise government I've taken the right path. In hindsight and with benefit of a great deal of experience, my decision to follow in the footsteps of the great models I had is also reaffirmed. Continuing my academic pursuits and my scientific endeavors while serving as a citizen-scientist was the right choice for me.

Outside of the Jasons, many people appreciated Drell's basic decency, concern for others, and keen ability to rise to any occasion. One of those was Rose Gottemoeller, an American diplomat and arms control negotiator who served as deputy secretary general of NATO from October 2016 until October 2019. She is now a lecturer at Stanford's Freeman Spogli Institute for International Studies and the Center for International Security and Cooperation. She was a corecipient with Drell of the Reykjavik Award in 2012, an occasion she remembers with particular clarity:

On the day of the award ceremony, I was a bit overwhelmed. I had a long speech that my Washington staff had prepared for me, but when the time came to accept the award, I set that speech aside and said a few words of appreciation. When Sid got up to receive his award, he launched into a self-written speech—the most articulate and heartfelt, but very sophisticated, disquisition on the importance of continued attention to the goals of negotiated arms reduction and control, the nonproliferation regime, and control over weapons of mass destruction, particularly nuclear weapons and fissile material. To this day, I feel a bit embarrassed to have been unable to reach those heights of rhetoric myself, but the high honor of the award left me wordless. Still, there was Sid, giving one of the most fantastic speeches I've ever heard, rising to the occasion 200 percent to make up for my shyness, and all to increase public awareness of the current state of weapons of mass destruction, arms control, and nonproliferation.

Acknowledging the significance of Drell's decision to combine his scientific and academic pursuits with government service, Pief Panofsky wrote the following in a 1988 letter to Drell on the occasion of his receipt of the Trimtab Award from the Buckminster Fuller Institute:

> It is extremely important that people who have achieved promi-
> nence in science are also discharging their responsibilities in cre-
> ating a better-informed community and leadership both in respect
> to the substance of science and in the values which have to be
> balanced between the benefits of science and the dangers which
> it creates. The public must understand and appreciate both the
> strength of scientists and the scientific process and the limits of
> what science can do. Understanding these values and their
> political implications is truly a matter of life and death when it
> comes to modern tools of war. You, Sid, are the leader in convey-
> ing all these factors to the general public, members and commit-
> tees of Congress, the Executive Branch, and scientists and leaders
> of other countries. . . . Your specialty is *building bridges* among
> all parties involved in the national and international security dia-
> logue. . . . In short, a peaceful world needs you.

⋁⋀⋀

CHAPTER 4

Declaration of Principle

Sid Drell never shied away from speaking up in the face of injustice or unfairness, particularly in advocating for Soviet physicist and dissident Andrei Sakharov, his friend and colleague. He also spoke out on issues of national defense, addressing top officials—right up to and including the president—if he felt they were pursuing a wrong course of action. With a sense of duty and considerable expertise concordant with his principles, he felt obliged to interject his informed opinion.

Drell himself singled out three instances that served as "points of pride"—a rare expression from one who never exhibited vanity. "The theme running through these incidents," Drell said, "is simply that I chose to be active in advocating for what I believed in. I spoke out for Andrei Sakharov; I spoke out for students; and in a letter to the president, I defended Robert Oppenheimer when he was under attack."

As for Drell's advocacy on behalf of Stanford students, an event in the spring of 1960 offers a dramatic example. The setting was San Francisco, May 1960, when the House Un-American Activities Committee was holding hearings to air concerns about links between communism and teaching in California universities. Drell recounted the circumstances as they unfolded:

In the first few days of the hearings, held in San Francisco City Hall, students were not permitted to attend; all seats were carefully allocated to ensure a friendly audience. But the sheriff of San Francisco County told some students that he personally would see to it that they would be seated at one of the hearings.

When the students from Stanford, Berkeley, and other local colleges showed up at the hearing on the morning of May 13, they approached the sheriff, who assured them again that they could attend the hearing after lunch. But on returning from the lunch adjournment and finding no available seats, these students began to protest. At a certain point, security personnel were called in and proceeded to turn their fire hoses on the students to force them down the central staircase of City Hall, causing serious injury to some of them.

At Stanford, three of us—Otis Pease, a history professor, Marshall Baker, a physics postdoc, and I—heard the news of the disturbance on the radio. Thereafter, we interviewed a group of the students involved and determined that the radio broadcast we had heard consisted solely of the police version of events. The three of us then wrote a letter, signed by at least one hundred professors—all the signatures we could gather in an afternoon— and delivered it to the *San Francisco Chronicle*. The letter was published the next day, and it generated big headlines.

In the office of the chief of the San Francisco Police Department was an administrative executive who, even though he was a Stanford alumnus, supported the police version of the narrative. He telephoned Wally Sterling, president of Stanford, to complain that our letter was one-sided, so Wally was obliged to meet with us—the three professors who instigated the letter's publication— and inform us of the complaint's suggested "bias" on our part. Wally gave us a little lecture, but we demurred, emphasizing that the police story had already been adequately told and documented and that the students' story—based on much credible evidence— provided a needed balance. It was apparent that Wally felt duty-bound to talk to us, but his heart wasn't in the pro forma lecture. In the end, no students were convicted for their role in the demonstrations, but the events at San Francisco City Hall came to be known as "Black Friday" and ushered in the US protest movement of the 1960s.

The Oppenheimer Case

Drell also defended J. Robert Oppenheimer, the theoretical physicist who played a crucial role in the development of the atomic bomb and then assumed an advisory role within the US Atomic Energy Commission. Oppenheimer eventually ran afoul of the FBI and the House Un-American Activities Committee and subsequently lost his security clearance. Drell recalled details of the incident and the disgraceful manner in which it was handled:

As head of the Los Alamos project, Oppenheimer ran the show, and he did it well. When told that he was suspected of being a communist, he requested a hearing.

Physicist Edward Teller, who had also worked on the Manhattan Project, had given testimony before the Atomic Energy Commission in April 1954 that he considered his former colleague Oppenheimer to be untrustworthy; it was Teller's testimony that prompted the commission's decision to suspend Oppenheimer's security clearance.

I thought the attacks were totally unjustified and wrote a letter to the president in Oppenheimer's defense.

Writing such a letter at the height of the Red Scare of the early fifties was a far more courageous act than penning a letter to the White House would normally be, but Drell had the courage of his convictions and was determined to express them to condemn this injustice. The matter was simply too important to ignore, especially

considering his standing in the physics community and his familiarity
with Oppenheimer's character.

Assessing Worldly Affairs

William Perry, who served as US secretary of defense in the Clinton
administration, offered more examples of Drell's bravery in speaking
truth to power. One instance dates back to the early 1970s, when
Perry and Drell found themselves acting as informal advisers to their
mutual friend Bud Wheelon, new deputy director of science and technology at the CIA.

"I had known Bud much earlier; he was a classmate of mine at
Stanford and had been Sid's classmate at MIT," Perry said. He recalled
times in that role when ambiguity was clarified and also when widely
held opinions were proven wrong:

> One interesting question in those days—shortly after the Rus-
> sians had launched their famous "monster bomb"—was what the
> Russians were going to do with it. It looked as though they were
> building a new ICBM, which we called the SS8. The Air Force
> declared—and had a very convincing set of forty or fifty charts as
> proof—that this new SS8 was a huge ICBM, designed to carry
> and launch the bomb. The reaction then, of course, was that the
> United States should build a big ICBM. Sid and I were two of
> the voices opposing the idea. We didn't think it was good for the
> United States to react in that way, and we didn't really believe
> the Russians were planning such a course of action. Still, the evi-
> dence was ambiguous. A year or so later, when the Russians
> paraded the SS8 in their May Day parade, we discovered, to our
> great joy, that it was a very small ICBM. Then all the talk of
> building a big ICBM to carry and launch a bomb just faded away.
>
> In 1977, I became the under secretary for research and engi-
> neering at the Department of Defense, and I looked for advice

in that area. One of the best sources of advice was a group of scientists known as the Jasons. Sid played a key role in the group and was among the three Jasons—Sid, Dick Garwin, and Charlie Townes—I consulted with most in those days. One of the things we disagreed on then was how to place the new MX missile. Sid and Dick wanted to place it in a shallow-submerged submarine in the ocean. I argued that it should be placed in an ICBM that could move around in several different silos. Despite our big disagreement, in the wisdom of hindsight, Sid and I concluded that we were both wrong. The best conclusion was not to base the missile at all, which is finally what happened, after we built the ICBM at considerable cost. The first time we had an arms agreement to reduce the number of ICBMs, the MX was the first thing to be eliminated. We don't hear much about the MX anymore, but it was a matter of great debate back in the seventies.

The Strategic Defense Debate

Drell had the enviable ability to take a stand, in opposition to those being pushed by the government or by many of his colleagues, without making enemies. One example is the Strategic Defense Initiative (SDI) of 1983, nicknamed Star Wars, in which President Reagan proposed the development of a system to shield the nation from attack and thereby render nuclear weapons obsolete. From the outset, Drell opposed the initiative, which was eventually abandoned as unattainable. His position seemingly aligned him with many Democrats and, therefore, pitted him against many Republicans. But no one ever accused Drell of taking a stand on partisan grounds because his reputation for integrity was beyond the taint of partisanship. He was widely regarded as being above such political bias, and this repute conferred a dependability that also endorsed him as expert-of-choice to White House administrations of both parties.

As Perry was also part of the SDI debate, he had this to offer:

When the great Strategic Defense Initiative debate was raised in the United States in the 1980s, Sid and I were on the same side of that argument, and we both wrote papers about it and discussed it in numerous conferences. My conclusion was that whatever was feasible in SDI was not desirable, and whatever was desirable in SDI was not feasible. Sid and I were fellow travelers in trying to fight the SDI battle. Our conclusion still holds today.

Shortly thereafter, I became secretary of defense and again turned to Sid for advice. The most prominent issue was the Comprehensive Nuclear-Test-Ban Treaty [CTBT]. President Clinton was being asked to sign the treaty and assigned me the task of bringing along the Joint Chiefs of Staff, which was no easy feat. To accomplish it, I enlisted the help of Jason and the lab directors. During our discussions, we got both the lab directors and Jason not only to make the argument in favor of the CTBT, but also to put forward the particular modification we could make that would render it completely acceptable to the Chiefs. The most important component of the modification was the Stockpile Stewardship Program, which even today is considered a great success and an important program in the United States.

In 2006, Perry and his late wife, Lee, moved to the Vi, a retirement community in Palo Alto where the Drells had relocated in the same year. This neighborly proximity led to opportunities for the couples to get to know each other on a more personal level, even as Perry and Drell continued to work together in a professional capacity on nuclear disarmament.

"Shortly after moving into the Vi, Sid and Harriet invited George Shultz and me, with our wives, to a dinner there," Perry recalled, adding details:

During that evening, I learned of Sid and George's plan to hold a conference at the Hoover Institution commemorating the

Reykjavik Summit on its twentieth anniversary. I was happy to be invited to attend that conference, which led shortly thereafter to the op-ed, "A World Free of Nuclear Weapons," that was published in the *Wall Street Journal* in January 2007. The op-ed outlined the current dangers of nuclear weapons and proposed a plan to reduce those dangers and, ultimately, to eliminate them. For the authors of the op-ed—Sid, George, Sam Nunn, Henry Kissinger, and me—it also meant the beginning of what others here refer to as the Gang of Five.

Regrettably, what began with great energy and enthusiasm and achieved significant results has faded away in the last few years. I believe we face greater dangers of a nuclear catastrophe occurring today than we faced during the Cold War. These are different dangers, but the threat of a nuclear catastrophe is greater. Because I believe that, I think we need the inspiration that Sid gives us even more today than ever. Remembering his sanity, his humanity, and his wisdom will help us educate people and energize efforts to reduce these dangers.

A Great Patriot, Plowing the Field

In fact, it was obvious to many that Drell typically played more of a behind-the-scenes role to the group commonly called the Gang of Four, whose public face presented the quartet of Shultz, Perry, Kissinger, and Nunn. Bob Peurifoy of Sandia Labs was one of many who was aware of Drell's significant yet discreet contributions, and remarked about the absence of recognition: "Although I don't personally know if the assembly of the four statesmen was spontaneous, I can guess that some interaction between Sid and George Shultz led to this joint alliance."

Peurifoy also echoed Perry's points about Drell's principled approach to questions of national security:

Sid and I keep up now and then to exchange points of view on this or that—test bans and so forth. He believes in striking a balance between advocating an appropriate weapons posture without over-doing it, and I think he's on the right track. He was instrumental in successfully supporting the Comprehensive Test Ban, not by making big waves but just by going about his work and plowing the field.

I know Sid took some blows from those who were—and still are—opposed to the Comprehensive Test Ban. Sid is a scientist who follows the rigors of the scientific method. With his reasoned approach, he just presented the facts, using believable arguments and whatever else worked to essentially isolate the doubters, who believed we should be testing more bombs forever. I admired that about him. No matter the consequences, Sid told the truth. Even, on occasion, when things got rough, he did not waver.

In sum, Sid is a great defender of a logical national security program. He doesn't believe that we should exceed a reasonable position regarding numbers and types of weapons. He believes in confronting the issues, addressing needs, and solving problems. He is not one to spend time on self-gratification. Diplomatic as Sid can be, he's also comfortable taking a firm stand, and he has a remarkable store of patience that makes him a good negotiator. I consider him to be a great man and patriot.

Drell found admirers among outsiders to the system as well. J. Bryan Hehir, a Roman Catholic priest and theologian and a professor at Harvard, worked with Drell on disarmament for many years:

I met Sid Drell through [national security expert] McGeorge "Mac" Bundy. The Catholic Bishops of the United States had just published the "Second Draft" of their pastoral letter on the nuclear age, and the draft had attracted broad attention.[1] Quite

---

1. The third and final draft of the letter, "The Challenge of Peace: God's Promise and Our Response," was approved at a meeting of the Catholic Bishops of the United States on May 3, 1983.

unexpectedly, I received a call from Bundy, who opened the discussion by saying, "I think the bishops have got it right and I'm willing to help in any way I can." His assistance became enormously helpful in multiple ways, including putting me in contact with Sid. I told Mac there was some apprehension among bishops about extending their moral analysis into the density of the technical issues in the nuclear debate of the 1980s. Mac said, "You need to get to know Sid Drell. He is the best person there is on the technical issues."

I pursued Sid, and so began one of the most significant friendships and working relationships of my life. Both our friendship and our work began immediately in 1982 and continued until Sid's illness in 2016. I came to know about this man's reputation among theoretical physicists and in the arms control community. Each of these dimensions of Sid's life became a source of insightful, wise, and lucid advice for the preparation of the final document, "The Challenge of Peace," in 1983. Far beyond that, and for decades, Sid's counsel guided US policy.

As a result of our collaboration, Sid invited me into the work of Stanford's Center for International Security and Arms Control. So began many annual visits to Stanford, during which I became acquainted, year by year, with the expansive range of contributions Sid made to the goals of taming the nuclear arms race and probing avenues to turn nuclear energy from the dangers of war to peaceful pursuits.

Andrei Sakharov: A Momentous Alliance

Russian physicist Andrei Sakharov and Sid Drell developed a unique and abiding friendship, one initiated at their first encounter. They shared a great apprehension about nuclear dangers, from which flowed their joint dedication to the control of nuclear arms and to bringing public attention—and some sanity—to the nuclear arms race. When Sakharov was forced to endure unimaginable privations at the hands of the Soviet government—including the KGB's theft of the only copy of his memoirs in retribution for his public criticism of nuclear programs—Drell counterchecked by championing Sakharov's cause in the public domain and by fighting for his freedom in letters of support published worldwide.

As a theoretical physicist, Sakharov played a crucial role in the development of the Soviet Union's nuclear weapons but grew concerned about the moral implications of his work, and thereafter became an activist for nonproliferation. After his ideas were published in the West, he was banned from military research. He also began speaking out on behalf of other activists who championed respect for human rights. In consequence, he endured deplorable treatment including arrest, force-feeding, internal exile, and constant harassment by the secret police.

No matter the cost to his life, Sakharov was unwavering in his mission. In a 1973 interview, Sakharov was asked by Swedish journalist Olle Stenholm, "You are doubtful that anything in general can be done to improve the system of the Soviet Union, yet you go ahead acting, writing declarations, protests—*why*?" Sakharov's response: "Well, there is a need to create ideals even when you can't see any route to achieve them, because if there are no ideals there can be no hope and then one would be completely in the dark, in a hopeless blind alley."[2] Drell, Sakharov's international ally, was equally stubborn in his determination to attract the world's decision makers to their shared causes.

Drell had visited the Soviet Union in 1959, but he met Sakharov for the first time while attending a scientific conference in Moscow in 1974. Drell recalled their first encounter:

It was a small gathering of Americans—maybe twenty-five of us—who had been invited by the Soviet Academy to convene

2. Council of Europe, Commissioner for Human Rights, *Andrei Sakharov and Human Rights* (Strasbourg: Council of Europe Publishing, 2010), 50–51.

on the topic of high energy physics. Sakharov walked in and approached me directly. He later told me that he had done so purposefully to establish contact. The ensuing conversation was difficult, because his English was not good and my Russian was worse, but we did have some overlap in German. He approached me as one he knew he could trust. At the end of our limited conversation he invited me to have dinner at his house. Since the two of us had what can be characterized as "pigeon-zoom" understandings of each other's country, we were glad for an opportunity to be enlightened further.

The timing coincided with Nixon and Kissinger's arrival in Moscow for what would be their last summit meeting with [Soviet leader Leonid] Brezhnev. The press was everywhere, but what made the evening's context quite sobering for me was the news that shortly before I arrived at Sakharov's apartment, the police had knocked on his door. Here I was, in this very modest apartment, an official visitor of a famous dissident, with access to the highest secrets and technology . . . how does one know when or if to be comfortable under these circumstances? I certainly didn't. Luckily, a translator, a young fellow scientist, showed up, so conversation flowed easily. Sakharov and I became fast and loyal friends, then and thereafter.

As with many events in Drell's life, this evening had a musical backdrop. The official visit from the police, Sakharov advised, had been prompted by complaints from nearby residents grumbling about "noisy neighbors who entertained many loud friends." They were referring to the previous night, Drell said, "when two lead singers from La Scala—in Moscow for a week at the Bolshoi—found their way to Sakharov's address and came to sing for him. It was the only gesture they could think of to offer their moral support. That was quite a tribute to a hero and, for me, a poignant tale of Sakharov's reach and significance to so many."

Andrei Sakharov and Elena Bonner, 1980: devoted to the end. A photo sent in a letter to Sid.

Drell continued:

At the dinner, I met both Sakharov's wife, Elena Bonner, and Elena's mother, Ruth Bonner, who was visiting them. Elena had been hospitalized for glaucoma and had been forced to bribe the hospital nurse in order to be released in time to see her mother. Ruth Bonner was a woman of great courage, too—yet another revolutionary in the family.

The press kept calling, interrupting us constantly for comment from Sakharov because Nixon and Kissinger were in town. Despite the interruptions, we managed to fill the evening with talk of significant issues.

And then, before the night was over, Sakharov announced that he would join in a one-week hunger strike—his first. Set to begin that very week, the strike was intended to underscore Sakharov's letter of protest to the heads of the US and Soviet governments at the Moscow summit and to support Elena's children, who were participants in the strike.

All of that took place in our first lengthy contact. It was clear to me that Sakharov trusted me; it took only seconds to realize that he was a man in whom I could place my trust, too. That first day of our acquaintance marked the beginning of a deeply personal, unforgettable friendship.

Two years later, I would go back to participate in a conference in Tbilisi, Georgia. At first, Sakharov wasn't allowed to attend, but he protested that as a member of the Russian Academy of Sciences, he was going, no matter what! The authorities relented and allowed him to attend but placed him in accommodations far below the first-class hotel arrangements enjoyed by all the other Russian hotshots.

Drell described sitting at the first of the conference's meetings and feeling a hand on his shoulder: Sakharov had come to greet him.

For the full week of the conference, I would have lunch with him and Elena in their hotel room. A couple of Georgian physicists, friends of Sakharov attending the conference, would join us in the lunches. Then, Sakharov would take his customary nap before the meetings reconvened; with his heart problems, he was never physically strong and he needed to rest between exertions.

The minute the people of Tbilisi became aware of Sakharov's presence in their city, they rushed to him, welcoming him as a hero, and informing him about political matters of great concern to them.

During the conference, I would ask the other attendees why Sakharov could not visit us in the States; after all, we had invited him numerous times. To bolster my argument, I cited the case of [writer Aleksandr] Solzhenitsyn, who was permitted to travel to America. I was told, "Solzhenitsyn is a religious mystic who would have very little impact in the West as opposed to Sakharov, who, as a traditional liberal, would be much more effective."

A Personal Conveyance

It was during this, their second encounter, that Sakharov asked if Drell would be willing to spirit out a letter to Elena's children in the United States. How could Drell refuse? But it was an undercover task that would require some guile, as Drell remembered:

Of course I agreed, took the letter with me, and forgot about it until I was on my way to the airport, where the possibility of being searched became a probability. I quickly hid the letter in my underwear, deciding that, in the event a search were imminent, I would demand to call my ambassador. In the end, airport security hurried me through as though nothing mattered, though they certainly knew who I was after my first meeting and subsequent public involvement with Sakharov. They did go through my suitcase with a fine-toothed comb, but they were focused on a book I'd brought along, Dostoevsky's *The Idiot*. They scrutinized its contents for a long time before determining that it was an innocent book. By then, it was time for my flight. They never did get to the bottom of my suitcase, where I had hidden writings from the West, which they would have found objectionable.

Sakharov, who received the Nobel Peace Prize in 1975, was also awarded the Joseph Prize for Human Rights by the Anti-Defamation League of B'nai B'rith in 1977. He was one of two recipients—the other being the then imprisoned Soviet Jewish activist Anatoly Shcharansky. Drell received the honor on Sakharov's behalf at a ceremony in Washington, DC. In the by-proxy acceptance speech, he took the opportunity to publicize incidents of current and ongoing abuse Sakharov was suffering at the hands of his government for

Drell with Sakharov (who admired his friend's distinctive taste in "circus jackets") at Stanford University in August 1989: equals united in perseverance for human rights and worldwide nuclear arms control.

publicly condemning officials' repressive, inhumane actions toward their own countrymen.

Drell then launched what would become a massive effort in leading the scientific community's support for Sakharov, exiled in Gorky and struggling to survive deplorable conditions there from 1980 through 1986. Throughout that time, Drell continued his public pleas for Sakharov's release, appealing to both Soviet and American politicians.

In 1985, Elena Bonner came to California and visited the Stanford campus. Drell recalled, "Much effort had gone into advance arrangements for medical treatments to address her health problems. Having just arrived, she took in the vistas of beautiful hills from Skyline to Portola Valley, and said wistfully, 'If only Andrei could see this! But this is the last you'll see of us because I am sure that when we get back, that will be the end of us. We will disappear.'"

Fortunately, Mikhail Gorbachev became leader of the Soviet Union and released Sakharov from exile in 1986. This was a triumph for many Sakharov supporters, Drell included, who, in his capacity as president of the American Physical Society (APS), sent a message of appreciation to the newly installed leader. Later, in retrospect, Drell revisited the memory of that occasion—and recalled others—when he seized opportunities to advocate for Sakharov while also broaching matters of great significance to both physicists:

Looking back [on my years as president of APS], I asked myself, what was my most satisfying experience in office? Without a doubt, it was sending a telegram to Soviet general secretary Mikhail Gorbachev on 19 December 1986—it was my last official communication as APS president—expressing my deep appreciation for his action in releasing Sakharov from internal exile in Gorky and permitting him to return to Moscow.

[Earlier,] in January 1986, the very first letter I signed as APS president was also addressed to Gorbachev. Noting that 1986 had started auspiciously with concrete new arms control initiatives between the United States and the Soviet Union following the Geneva summit conference of 1985, I expressed hopes for progress during the year in efforts to reduce the threat of a nuclear holocaust.

At the same time, I expressed my deep personal concern for the situation of Sakharov and asked if it was too much to hope that during 1986 we might see his return to the normal privileges of Soviet citizens in Moscow. I pointed out that many of the issues that the general secretary was now emphasizing as policy goals were the same ones that Sakharov had been supporting and speaking out in support of for many years. These included emphasizing the great importance of arms control to lead us away from the risk of nuclear holocaust, of keeping weapons out of space, and of ceasing nuclear weapons tests. I said that Sakharov, who together with I. E. Tamm wrote the fundamental paper on the principle of the *tokamak* [a magnetic confinement device used in research toward a fusion reactor], could contribute importantly to further cooperation between our countries in research to harness fusion as a peaceful source of energy.

Finally, I emphasized that in addition to benefiting from Sakharov's voice toward achieving these shared goals, the Soviet Union should honor its greatest theoretical physicist, not isolate him from colleagues and thereby impede his physics research.

So it gave me great pleasure to close my term in office by being able to see this come to pass.[3]

Father-Son Adventures

Along with the rest of the family, Daniel Drell had enjoyed frequent travels with his father, including their visit to the Soviet Union in 1987. Weighing in on the Sakharov-Drell partnership, Daniel offered a unique perspective on his father's relationship with Sakharov and provided observations on conditions in the Soviet Union at the time:

One terrific experience of my life happened when, during a week in 1987, my father and I spent time in the Soviet Union, a visit with Sakharov included. It was in 1974 that my father and Sakharov had first met, a few years after the publication of

---

3. Reproduced from Sidney D. Drell, "Thoughts of a Retiring APS President," *Physics Today* 40, no. 8 (August 1987): 62, with the permission of the American Institute of Physics.

Sakharov's groundbreaking book *Progress, Coexistence, and Intellectual Freedom.*[4] Thereafter, they had become close friends.

It was especially exciting to witness Sakharov open his apartment door to us and greet my father with an exuberant cry of "Seed-ney!" and then to observe as they, in Russian style, kissed each other's cheeks.

Another memorable part of the trip actually began unfolding at Kennedy Airport just before we boarded our flight for Moscow. I purchased a copy of *Time* magazine that included a photo of Mathias Rust, the German teenager who had flown across Eastern Europe and landed in Red Square. The photo had been taken a few days before by tourists in Moscow. As we were going through customs in Moscow, I thought that this magazine would be the first thing the customs agents would confiscate, but they only asked if we were carrying any videotapes. I wondered if my father's special status was the reason they didn't bother with the magazine, but later, it would be cause for some unusual exchanges.

A few days into our trip, my father and I visited the Soviet Academy of Sciences and met with the son of Peter Kapitza, a Nobel laureate physicist. When I mentioned that I had with me the issue of *Time*, academician Vladimir Gribov, one of the Soviet Union's most accomplished physicists and a Sakharov supporter, jumped from his chair, took three steps toward me, hand extended, and asked, "May I see it?" Clearly, everyone knew about the Mathias Rust incident, but the KGB had managed to suppress the photographs. For the second, and final, time, the magazine became a matter of pressing interest when we visited Kapitza's dacha a few days later. I handed it to one of the physicists there and never again laid eyes on it. I found the exchanges prompted by the magazine of great interest as I personally witnessed just

---

4. New York: W. W. Norton, 1968.

how significant Western coverage of the incident was to the Russians, there and then.

Keeping Sakharov's Memory Alive

Drell relished both his personal and his professional connections with Sakharov and expressed his great enthusiasm and gratitude for the extraordinary experiences the two had shared.

Beyond friendship, I also take personal pride in the fact that Andrei and I are members of the same scientific community. As theoretical physicists, we are fellow members of the crew on that great adventure voyage of the human mind searching to discover what we are made of. We share this passion to understand nature. What are the elementary building blocks on the submicroscopic scale of distances hundreds of millions to billions of times smaller than the size of the atom? What are the forces that glue together the building blocks, or elementary constituents, of nature into the protons and neutrons and other forms of matter that we actually see in the laboratory?[5]

Serving as Sakharov's advocate included fostering communications with others who could join in the effort. David Holloway, professor of international history, senior fellow emeritus at the Freeman Spogli Institute of International Studies, and faculty member at Stanford's Center for International Security and Cooperation, described how Drell helped him get in touch with Sakharov:

I've known Sid since I came to Stanford in 1983. CISAC had just been set up as a center, and Sid was the codirector with John Lewis. I came on a three-year visit, very quickly got involved

5. Andrei Sakharov, Sidney D. Drell, and Sergei P. Kapitza, eds., *Sakharov Remembered* (Melville, NY: American Institute of Physics, 1991), 102–3.

in one of Sid's projects, and ended up coauthoring a book with him on the Strategic Defense Initiative. The two people who started the project were Sid and Phil Farley, who had retired after years in government working on arms control issues at the State Department and the Atomic Energy Commission. They asked me to write a report on the Soviet Union's response to Star Wars, and we published a CISAC report that a publisher picked up.

It was as an analyst of the technical aspects of security policy that I first came to know Sid. Throughout our collaborations, then and thereafter, what struck me was Sid's focus, which was connected to the power of his intellect. I've had conversations with him wherein he would say, "No, that's not worth looking at. You'll only get lost."

I was writing about the history of the Soviet atomic project when Sid offered to put me in touch with Andrei Sakharov. That was in 1987, just after Sakharov had returned from exile in Gorky. I was in Moscow at a conference and made the arrangement to see Sakharov at his apartment. I remember being at his door, thinking to myself, "What am I doing here? Here's a man with very important things to do and I've come to inquire about his involvement in the nuclear project." But within thirty seconds, Sakharov's immense personal charm had me feeling totally at ease. We talked for about three hours, and he seemed quite interested in discussing the topic. Maybe it was a distraction from the many other concerns he had.

It's interesting that Sid became friendly with Andrei Sakharov. In the time I spent with Sakharov, I was impressed by the similarity of his mind to Sid's—specifically, the ability to focus. With Sakharov, as with Sid, I'd ask a question and wouldn't get a quick answer. Some brilliant people can respond quickly; these two were like lighthouses. They thought about the question, sent out the "inquiry beam," which moved about, then focused, until . . . *there!* . . . the question was illuminated and the response clear.

Atlantic City High School graduate Drell, 1942, headed to Princeton and the instruction (and lifelong influence) of titans in the physics world.

Harriet Stainback, c. 1951, upon entering the working world as a Russian language instructor at the Armed Forces Security Agency, precursor to today's National Security Agency.

Sid, Elena Bonner, and Andrei Sakharov in Tbilisi, Georgia, 1974: in a stolen moment of levity, free from the world stage and matters of great magnitude.

On a hike in Banff National Park, c. 1980.

The coveted SLAC softball game trophy featuring a record of historic rivalry: over the course of nearly two decades, Experimentalists sweep Theorists 17–1, contrary to their matched firepower in the lab.

(L to R) Drell, George Shultz, a translator, and Mikhail Gorbachev at Stanford in 1990. Sid, blending scientific know-how with diplomacy on an international scale.

President Clinton greets Drell, a member of the President's Foreign Intelligence Advisory Board, 1993.

Lecturing at the Institute of Theoretical and Experimental Physics, Moscow, October 1998, upon receiving the first Pomeranchuk Prize for Theoretical Physics research.

Drell and George Shultz: Princeton alums in their mascot's colorful finery, two tigers of different stripes, but allied strategists for nuclear disarmament.

Daniel and Lois Drell in Moscow, 2014.

Persis Drell and Jim Welch, cross-country skiing at Jackson Hole, 2017.

Joanna Drell and husband, David Routt: Italophiles, at Rome's Trevi Fountain, 2008.

President Obama confers upon Drell the National Medal of Science, 2013.

Drell, George Shultz, and Lucy Shapiro on the occasion of Drell and Shapiro receiving the National Medal of Science Award in Washington, DC, 2013.

Daniel, Persis, Sid, and Joanna Drell with President Obama in the Oval Office, 2013.

Sid and Harriet at their Vi apartment, Palo Alto, 2006.

The cosmic event captured in this illustration inspired the overarching theme of "Time's Arrow," Lenora Ferro's poetic eulogy for Dr. Drell (see pages 150–51).

Adding different perspectives on the Drell-Sakharov accord, sense of kinship, and respective influences on the world stage are two other people familiar with the historic relationship: Malvin Ruderman and David Hamburg.

Ruderman, a veteran of the Corona project, could see that Drell's championing of Sakharov influenced the wider community of physicists. In his words, "Sid played a truly memorable role in protecting contacts with fellow physicists in the USSR during the Cold War. In the case of Andrei Sakharov in Gorky, Sid's efforts to focus outside attention on Sakharov's plight emboldened many and became important in even more ways than simply advocating for a single cause." Hamburg, president emeritus of Carnegie Corporation of New York, met Drell at Stanford in 1957. He recalled, "Sid made distinguished achievements in basic physics and could have kept on in that field for the rest of his career. Instead, he threw himself into the most difficult world problems for years. In one extraordinary accomplishment during the Cold War, Sid established a deep friendship with Andrei Sakharov. This development in alliance is, in my mind, the most dramatic of breakthroughs during that era. For Sid, it's one of the greatest compliments of his life that Sakharov trusted him. Their communication over those years made a great difference."

By 1988, some progress had been made on nuclear disarmament when Sakharov finally came to the United States. The visit was a victory for which Drell could be credited. Through his public statements at various international events, he had pointedly demanded, "Why not allow Sakharov to travel?"

As Drell remembered it, "I greeted Andrei in Washington, where I addressed the meeting of the National Academy of Sciences, welcoming him and inducting him into the membership. Then, in 1989, Andrei was allowed to attend a conference at Stanford, after which George Shultz hosted a post-conference dinner in his honor. Later, I received a letter from him—one of extreme sadness—saying that he knew it was the end, and we would never see him again."

Drell, Andrei Sakharov, and Pief Panofsky on the occasion of Sakharov's
visit to Stanford for the International Lepton-Photon Symposium, 1989:
a triumvirate whose combined principled brilliance changed our world.

When Sakharov died, in December 1989, it was widely held that the
world had lost one of its beacons of truth and justice for humanity—a
global loss of immeasurable proportions. For Drell, Sakharov's death
resonated on many levels. And thereafter, he would seek out and take
opportunities to promote the continuance of Sakharov's mission,
which the Russian had pursued so bravely until his death.

One year after Sakharov's death, Drell and Lev Okun, of the
Institute of Theoretical and Experimental Physics in Moscow, contributed an article to the August 1990 issue of *Physics Today* in which

they wrote: "Sakharov's voice is now sorely missed, but his spirit continues to energize and guide the quest he led for more than two decades—the quest for justice, human dignity and freedom everywhere in this world."[6]

In *Sakharov Remembered: A Tribute by Friends and Colleagues*, Drell wrote, "As much as any scientist I know, Andrei Sakharov has understood the special obligation of the scientific community to alert society to the implications of the products of scientific advances and to assist society in shaping the applications of these advances in beneficial directions."[7]

In 1991, Drell participated in the First Sakharov International Congress, "Peace, Progress, Human Rights," which Elena Bonner convened in Moscow. Present among a crowd of international representatives were Soviet president Gorbachev; Boris Yeltsin, chairman of the Russian Republic Supreme Soviet; and other participants, as Bonner noted in her address, "from different worlds, representing different professions and social positions, different parties and movements, different views."

Sakharov and Drell had many things in common. But if there is a trait to be singled out, it was their shared faith in humankind. Both men reached beyond science and delved into the arts, music, and philosophy. Neither man could turn his back on the ethical duties inherent in science. Both felt privileged and regarded life as a gift to be shared through efforts and achievements in the world of physics and expanded thereafter via the bully pulpits available to them as a result of those successes and the consequences thereof.

---

6. Sidney Drell and Lev Okun, "Andrei Dmitrievich Sakharov," *Physics Today* 43, no. 8 (August 1990), 36.

7. Sakharov, Drell, and Kapitza, *Sakharov Remembered*, 87.

CHAPTER 5

∿

The Hoover Institution
and the Gang of Four

Following an illustrious career at Stanford and SLAC, many years of public service, and numerous awards and honors, Sidney Drell could have settled into well-deserved retirement in 1998. Instead, he began a new chapter at the Hoover Institution, where he spent the last eighteen years of his life and career as a senior fellow. Founded in 1919 by Stanford University alumnus Herbert Hoover, the Hoover Institution on War, Revolution, and Peace was established on the Stanford campus as a library and archives dedicated to the study of war, its causes and effects, and the paths to peace. By the 1950s its purpose was reimagined by its founder as a public-policy institution committed to expanding peace, prosperity, and freedom around the world.

"One of the high points of my life," Drell recalled, "was set into motion when George Shultz returned to Stanford in early 1989." Shultz was a Princeton alumnus and a Marine Corps veteran who had already served in various positions in academia and government when he originally came to Stanford as a fellow at the Center for Advanced Study in the Behavioral Sciences from 1968 to 1969. He then served in the Nixon and Reagan administrations, where he held four cabinet positions, including that of secretary of state during the Reagan administration. After his government service and a period spent in the private sector as president of Bechtel Corporation, he returned to Stanford in 1989 as a professor at the Graduate School of Business and a distinguished fellow at the Hoover Institution.

A Ready Bond

Shultz had heard Drell's name repeated so often through the intelligence grapevine that when he left government service and returned to Stanford, he immediately sought him out:

> Putting my relationship with Sid into the context of my time as secretary of state, I was, of course, aware of nuclear issues and I had some contact with the CIA, but I wasn't up on the intricate details.
>
> At State, I inherited two colleagues who were extremely helpful. One was Jim Timbie, a physicist who had been associated with Sid Drell at Stanford before going to Washington, where he worked on arms control issues. The other was Paul Nitze, a famous Cold Warrior who was very experienced in Soviet affairs. Jim and Paul were my educators and consultants as I worked on our nuclear agenda with the Soviet Union.
>
> A strong component of the agenda was arms control. In the Reagan administration, we deviated from the past in several ways. We advocated for a large-scale reduction in nuclear weapons and we discarded the concept of détente that had characterized earlier times. The idea of détente was, "We're here, they're there, that's life, and we'll do the best we can." We said, "No; we're here, they're not going to be there forever, and they're weaker than is thought." We were willing to work for change. The third deviation we pursued was the concept of linkage; that is, if something goes wrong in a particular subject matter area, everything else is affected. We didn't buy it.
>
> Jim and Paul kept referring to someone named Sid Drell. On all sorts of sensitive issues, they were forever quoting Sid, and I

could tell that what Sid thought made a lot of sense. I found it all quite interesting. Worthy of note is the fact that Jim, a Sid protégé, was very effective in the State Department. He was helpful to me, and I could see that he was respected by everybody as both a fine physicist and a sensible, straightforward person. In those ways, he is Sid Drell–like. Today, Jim occupies Sid's former office at Hoover; it's an appropriate passing down to someone so worthy.

As I heard more about Sid Drell, I learned that he didn't think much of the president's Strategic Defense Initiative. I thought the press on that initiative was overblown; still, it turned out to be an absolutely key bargaining chip with the Soviet Union. So, whatever its merits in the eyes of US scientists, the Soviets perceived it as powerful and were willing to bargain a lot for it.

Sid had views about our reduction initiatives, and my memory is that he was among those who supported the idea that we should reduce nuclear weapons. In the past, the negotiations had been about limiting them—witness the Strategic Arms Limitation Treaty. There was a sharp difference in the Reagan approach, and Sid reinforced it.

Having heard so often about Sid when I was in office, I decided to phone him when I came back to Stanford in 1989, and we made a lunch date. As we talked about nuclear arms reduction and a wide range of other subjects, I realized immediately that Sid was someone who was not only interesting but also fun to be with. We just clicked.

Of this first meeting over lunch, Drell recalled:

Once we met up and lunch was under way, it didn't take long for us to discover how much we had in common, a Princeton alma mater included. As it happened, I mentioned the fact that I had drafted a letter to the Princeton administration to protest their proposed elimination of the senior thesis requirement. George shared my sentiments about the importance of the thesis in the Princeton education and joined me in signing the letter.

The Princeton letter would be the kick-off leading to years of work by Drell and Shultz on issues of common interest, their friendship deepening along the way.

Shultz became keenly aware that Drell, in addition to his years of research and teaching in physics, was highly respected in scientific and governmental circles for his work on matters of national security. Recognizing him as a potentially important ally, Shultz offered him a post as a senior fellow at Hoover when Drell retired in 1998 as emeritus professor at SLAC. Of the offer tendered, Drell said it took "no more than five seconds" to accept.

As a senior fellow at Hoover, Drell continued his push for the elimination of nuclear weapons as part of Shultz's crusade for disarmament, giving lectures, participating in conferences, and writing and editing books. With decades of combined experience in arms control issues, theirs would prove an effective partnership in the cause of nuclear security. Using Hoover as a base, and occupying offices just down the hall from one another, Shultz and Drell had immediate daily access for the exchange of ideas. Shultz recalled:

We clicked right from that first lunch and enjoyed each other's company from then on. Sid's door was always open to me and mine to him. Often I'd arrive at Hoover, pop my head into Sid's office, and ask for a translation, in layman's terms, of some physics material I'd read in the morning papers. "Hey, Sid, what about this?" He'd explain it, enlightening me with his easy style, and then he'd laugh.

Our tradition of regular lunches together developed into a monthly lunch club when we invited Lucy Shapiro, a developmental biologist at Stanford, to join us. Later, our group grew to include [Stanford University president] Gerhard Casper and others. Our conversation topics were never preordained. Whatever came up, came up, and we each had our say.

Sid served on government panels that oversaw the national labs, so he was well informed about their activities, particularly at Lawrence Livermore National Laboratory. He admired the work of the labs and weighed in on management issues. Sid was very helpful in making meetings meaningful for me at the Livermore and Los Alamos labs. Going on my own would have been unproductive because they could have told me anything and I wouldn't have known what to make of it. With Sid present, they were obliged to "talk straight," so Sid was always by my side when I visited the labs. That resulted in wonderful insights because Sid would ask questions in layman's terms that allowed me to comprehend them, just as he demanded answers from them that would be understandable to me.

Another keen perspective on the Drell-Shultz duo comes from a friend to both, journalist Jim Hoagland, who addressed members and guests at the American Nuclear Society's Eisenhower Award ceremony in Washington, DC, in November 2015. Hoagland took the opportunity to highlight the productive teamwork and personal relationship between Drell and Shultz, the first recipients of the award:

It is characteristic of George Shultz that one of his first actions on arriving at Stanford in 1989 was reaching out to Sid Drell, a visionary nuclear scientist he did not know but had heard a great deal about in Washington, particularly from the legendary defense policy expert Paul Nitze. You would not think that Nitze, known as a Reagan conservative and consummate Cold Warrior, and Sid Drell, whose political leanings were more on the Democratic and liberal side, would make natural soulmates, but they deeply respected each other's intellect, integrity, and love of country. When George and Sid met for lunch in early 1989, the conversation quickly turned to their mutual concern about the menace of nuclear weapons. George has been heard to observe that Sid "actually understood how these damned things work."

In temperament and character, George Shultz and Sid Drell reinforce each other's strengths. George is a lifelong study in integrity, a Marine who has lived by his code of honor and by his word. Sid is a man of science who is passionate about his beliefs and values. Together they have advanced our common understanding of what must be done to preserve human existence.[1]

Complementary Colleagues

The focus of Drell's and Shultz's work had a natural balance. Shultz had the public-policy experience, having been a key figure in the Reykjavik negotiations between Reagan and Gorbachev, and Drell could weigh in with his scientific knowledge of nuclear weapons. Both were tacticians, and each could call upon wide networks of colleagues at Stanford and beyond. Drell's connections to national and international scientists, including his long acquaintance with Andrei Sakharov, dovetailed nicely with Shultz's national and international stature.

Drell was determined after Sakharov's death in 1989 to honor the Russian and keep the nuclear weapons dialogue from fading in the public eye. In Shultz he found a steadfast ally. Sakharov's legacy came to assume a central role in their mission to reenergize the nuclear weapons debate. In 1999, for the tenth anniversary of Sakharov's death, they organized a conference at Stanford to discuss the historic and current relevance of Sakharov's advocacy for international peace, nuclear arms control, and human rights.

In this, as in all of their efforts, the Reykjavik summit loomed large in discussions about nuclear nonproliferation. Reagan and Gorbachev had each, in different ways, called for the elimination of the nuclear

---

1. Jim Hoagland, remarks, Eisenhower Award Panel, American Nuclear Society Winter Meeting, Washington, DC, November 9, 2015.

At the Sakharov Conference at Stanford, 1999:
tireless advocate for nuclear arms sanity, invoking
the legacy of colleague and friend Sakharov for
added momentum worldwide.

threat, but they had been unable to reach agreement. Drell recalled his
reaction to the summit at the time:

> People like me have talked about getting rid of nuclear weap-
> ons all our lives. I remember being in Washington the day the
> Reykjavik summit concluded. Because I never thought in 1986
> that we could rid the world of these weapons, I did not share
> the sense of disappointment that others felt after the summit
> ended. The Berlin Wall still stood, and the Cold War would go
> on for another five years, but the leaders of the two superpowers
> had declared their resolve to reduce nuclear weapons. Until
> then, no one had said politically that we would reduce these
> weapons. Reagan and Gorbachev had just vowed to make it
> happen. For people like me, it was something to celebrate.

And thereafter, in conjunction with Shultz, Drell considered how important it was to parlay the promise of the Reagan-Gorbachev declaration into further gains in the nuclear-arms-reduction effort. As Drell put it:

> We had made progress [in nuclear arms reduction] from a maximum of seventy thousand or so nuclear weapons in the world to around fifteen thousand—though what good does that do? Even with a small fraction of weapons remaining, the threat continues; if they're deployed, there ain't gonna be much of life left! So George and I started searching for ways to continue addressing the great problems in the nuclear weapons realm that remained to be solved.

Shultz and Drell recognized that they had to remind and convince people of the overwhelming danger of nuclear weapons. In strategizing their moves, Drell said, "We also realized that persuading countries to work toward the elimination of nuclear weapons *step by step* would require a political effort. With the addition of three seasoned statesmen—Henry Kissinger, Sam Nunn, and Bill Perry—our group had the essential credibility, expertise, and clout for developing a series of steps toward a nuclear-free world. With George as the fourth statesman, the group came to be dubbed the 'Gang of Four.'"

Drell's reasoning for the alliance with these political stalwarts was that "these men of renown had served with great dignity and had earned respect for their efforts to make and keep America strong. Scholars, or a scientist–arms controller like me, wouldn't have the influence, access, or cachet that these four enjoyed worldwide."

As the twentieth anniversary of the 1986 Reykjavik summit approached, Drell and Shultz decided it would be an auspicious moment to host a serious discussion on lessons learned from that historic event. So the Gang of Four (and Drell, a silent fifth, by choice) convened a small group of scholars, scientists, and diplomats on October 11–12, 2006, at the Hoover Institution for a conference—"Implications of the Reykjavik Summit on Its Twentieth Anniversary"—where they discussed the potential for reviving the Reagan-Gorbachev vision.

A significant result of that conference was an editorial, "A World Free of Nuclear Weapons," written by Shultz, Perry, Kissinger, and Nunn, with Drell as a silent contributor. Published in the *Wall Street Journal* on January 4, 2007, the authors called for rekindling the hope expressed at the Reykjavik summit. Shultz recalled this sequence of events:

In 2006, we held a conference at Hoover to mark the twentieth anniversary of the Reykjavik summit. After that meeting, Sid and I met with Bill Perry and Sam Nunn and we developed a statement, which I took to the Bohemian Grove to show Henry Kissinger. His reaction was, "This is very important." I admitted that the statement was still a work in progress and invited him to join in the effort, which he did. As Sid had suspected from the very beginning, our *Wall Street Journal* op-ed of January 4, 2007, hit the world like a lightning bolt. In his typical style, Sid declined to add his name to the piece as a contributing author despite the fact that he had made a huge contribution to it. Among other things, he added essential reassurance that we'd gotten the science right.

The article described how the Reykjavik summit had successfully changed the complexion of the nuclear weapons debate, decreasing the threat in unexpected and remarkable ways and creating a wave of increased interest in nuclear security. "Without the bold vision," the authors wrote, "the actions will not be perceived as fair or urgent. Without the actions, the vision will not be perceived as realistic or possible." And then, a thoughtful response from none other than Mikhail Gorbachev, entitled "The Nuclear Threat," appeared in the *Wall Street Journal* on January 31, 2007, propelling the discussion even further. He wrote: "We must put the goal of eliminating nuclear weapons back on the agenda, not in a distant future but as soon as possible. It links the moral imperative—the rejection of such weapons from an ethical standpoint—with the imperative of assuring security. It is becoming clearer that nuclear weapons are no longer a means of achieving security; in fact, with every passing year they make our security more precarious."

Hoagland recalled that seminal op-ed by the Gang of Four (plus Drell):

> This and subsequent articles brought the topic of nuclear disarmament into the mainstream of American politics and discourse. These articles and the outreach that surrounded them involved the establishment in a cause that had been largely left to fringe political movements. They connected the political establishment to those in the scientific community—like Sid Drell and Andrei Sakharov—who had long been grappling with the immense dangers that often come with scientific and technological advances.
>
> I confess to approaching what George and Sid were proposing with a journalistic frame of mind ranging from agnosticism to skepticism. But I quickly discovered at a Hoover conference on building a new system of deterrence to replace mutually assured destruction that they were deadly serious about this work and were prepared to do the heavy lifting needed to create the conditions that would permit nations to abandon their nuclear arsenals. These are not romanticists pushing illusionary, illogical disarmament schemes but clear-eyed realists responding to growing threats of catastrophic damage to the globe and the human race.

"Reykjavik Revisited"

Drell, Shultz, Perry, Kissinger, and Nunn, in collaboration with the Nuclear Threat Initiative, the nonprofit organization Nunn cofounded to develop policies to prevent the use of nuclear weapons, seized further opportunity by convening a second conference, "Reykjavik

Revisited: Steps Toward a World Free of Nuclear Weapons," October 24–25, 2007, at the Hoover Institution. The event brought together senior scholars, scientific experts on nuclear issues, and representatives from six past administrations.

The results of this collaborative work produced impressive gains in worldwide notice and resolve, including an opinion piece, "Toward a Nuclear-Free World," by Shultz, Perry, Kissinger, and Nunn, published in the *Wall Street Journal* on January 15, 2008. They concluded, "In some respects, the goal of a world free of nuclear weapons is like the top of a very tall mountain. From the vantage point of our troubled world today, we can't even see the top of the mountain, and it is tempting and easy to say we can't get there from here. But the risks from continuing to go down the mountain or standing pat are too real to ignore. We must chart a course to higher ground where the mountaintop becomes more visible."

Shultz, Drell, and James Goodby, former ambassador and disarmament negotiator for three administrations, were invited by Norway's minister of foreign affairs to attend an international conference on nuclear disarmament in Oslo in February 2008. Shultz delivered the keynote speech, followed by Drell and Goodby's report on the 2007 Hoover-NTI conference.

Then, on March 27, 2009, Gorbachev spoke at President Reagan's alma mater, Eureka College, in Illinois, and said of the Reykjavik summit, "It was not a failure; it was a breakthrough, because for the first time we looked beyond the horizon." In a 2016 interview, Shultz echoed that sentiment, saying, "The summit succeeded in turning the arms race on its head. It was a watershed event in our relations."

In April 2009, US president Barack Obama and Russian Federation president Dmitry Medvedev issued a joint statement committing their two countries to the goal of a nuclear weapons–free world. The following month, Obama invited the Gang of Four to meet with him in the Oval Office.

"We had a very spirited, constructive dialogue," Shultz recalled. At a press conference following the meeting, he said, "We think of the

The Gang of Four—plus one: (L to R) Drell, Sam Nunn, Henry Kissinger, William Perry, and George Shultz at the Hoover Institution, January 14, 2013— a powerful alliance for the elimination of nuclear weapons.

endeavor [to reduce the nuclear threat] and ourselves as nonpartisan in this instance. The subject has no partisan content . . . and ought to be discussed and argued on its merits."

Then, in September 2009, Obama once again called on the Gang of Four, inviting them to join him at the United Nations, where he would be the first US president to chair a meeting of the Security Council. The resulting resolution, passed unanimously by the body's fifteen nations, resolved "to create the conditions for a world without nuclear weapons . . . in a way that promotes international stability . . . based on the principle of undiminished security for all."[2] The impetus prompted by Drell and Shultz in the corridors of the Hoover Institution had led directly to this pledge.

---

2. United Nations Security Council Resolution 1887, adopted unanimously on September 24, 2009.

In the ensuing years, members of the Hoover group and the Gang of Four—plus Drell—would continue to publish articles and essays in the national and foreign media, keeping the topic and debate about nuclear weapons issues a matter of widespread interest. These included two additional essays in the *Wall Street Journal* by Shultz, Perry, Kissinger, and Nunn: "How to Protect Our Nuclear Deterrent" on January 19, 2010, and "Deterrence in the Age of Nuclear Proliferation" on March 7, 2011.

Memorable Soirées

But it wasn't all work for the Gang of Four and their colleagues. There were also gala dinner parties hosted by the Shultzes at their campus digs. George's tradition was to ensure that the conversation at these gatherings was engaging and enlightening. One memorable evening in 2012 included a discussion about the breaking news of the Higgs boson's discovery. Drell, of course, was expected to take the floor. Years later, he was ebullient as he revisited the circumstances and unforgettable dialogue of that evening:

> The Higgs boson discovery accomplished a huge advance in our understanding of how we evolved from the Big Bang. It confirmed many ideas about the general theory of relativity and the origin of the universe. Henry Kissinger was eager to know why that was important. I stressed the fundamental value in having a deeper understanding of how the universe began expanding and is now radiating gravitational waves we can see. Learning about that evolution is valuable because we have no data from before the Big Bang, so this development poses opportunities to address questions about the pre–Big Bang era—some 13.8 billion years ago—and search for possible answers.
>
> This effort is just as important as trying to understand how simple molecules of DNA somehow or other found themselves in a combination that led to the emergence of life. We don't

understand either of these puzzles, but we now have fundamental questions to which we can look for answers in this new
discovery that will allow us to pose more questions about it and
search for answers.

My explanation prompted a lively discussion. Henry asked
probing questions, and I, apparently, gave answers that could be
understood. He seemed riveted, and there was not a word said,
other than mine, for about twenty minutes. Because Henry was
asking, I was not about to yield the floor until I'd answered him
as fully as possible, given the circumstances. I've known Henry
for many years, but that evening was the only time I've ever had
the opportunity for a deep intellectual conversation with him.

Later, when word of that dinner conversation had made the rounds,
Drell shyly summed up reactions from others with this gratifying
observation: "I've learned since then that many guests that evening,
including Jim Hoagland and Phil Taubman, were equally as enthralled
by the discussion as Henry and I were."

Returning to matters concerning nuclear weapons, Drell cited details
of joint efforts that continued: "Fast forward to 2014, twenty-five
years after Sakharov's death, and things were not going well in the
nuclear arms arena." There were concerns about the longevity of
Sakharov's influence. "George and I decided to convene a group of
scholars, historians, military commanders, theologians, scientists, technological entrepreneurs, and other opinion makers to discuss the ways
that Sakharov influenced the dialogue surrounding nuclear security.
We hoped to investigate how he had become an exemplar for public
scrutiny of political policy making in matters of great consequence to
his country, to the world at large—to our very humanity."

The resulting conference, "Andrei Sakharov: The Conscience of
Humanity," took place December 10–11, 2014, at the Hoover
Institution, marking the twenty-fifth anniversary of the Russian's
death. In 2015, the proceedings of that conference were published
by Hoover in a book of the same title, edited by Drell and Shultz.

The volume contains the papers presented by the conference participants, whose varied fields of expertise brought new perspectives to the consideration of Sakharov's influence on current issues, particularly nuclear security and human rights.

Drell and Shultz continued to promote Sakharov's legacy. In 2015, *Foreign Affairs* published "The Man Who Spoke Truth to Power: Andrei Sakharov's Enduring Relevance," by Drell, Shultz, and journalist Hoagland. In this essay, the authors asked—and proposed answers to—the question: "How should today's thinkers and policy makers deal with contemporary and future nuclear threats?"[3]

Later, Hoagland summarized the influences that united Drell and Sakharov:

> There are many parallels between Sid and Andrei Sakharov. Both are premier scientists; they both make a relationship between human rights and the progress of science; and they share serious qualms about the development of nuclear weapons, particularly thermonuclear weapons. From the stories Sid has told me about him and from what I've read, Sakharov also had a deeply humane approach to science. He looked at the good as well as the bad, both of which scientific progress inevitably brings, assessing the trade-offs and weighing the balances. Obvious in both men, too, is a deep concern for the fate of humanity. They write about it and underscore the dangers that nuclear weapons present to humankind's survival—a concern they hold in common, probably because they know intimately these terrible weapons. Then, there's the matter of an implicit trust between them, evidenced in Sid's surreptitious spiriting of Sakharov's letter out of the Soviet Union.

---

3. Sidney D. Drell, Jim Hoagland, and George P. Shultz, "The Man Who Spoke Truth to Power: Andrei Sakharov's Enduring Relevance," *Foreign Affairs*, June 25, 2015.

Meanwhile, in 2013, the "Shultz Corner" on the second floor of the Herbert Hoover Memorial Building at Hoover welcomed a new member, General James Mattis, who arrived after retiring from his position as commander of US Central Command. Soon into Mattis's tenure at Hoover, Drell took the younger colleague under his wing. The two formed an immediate bond and were often found in discussion in Drell's corner office.

About the new member of the coterie, Drell said, "These past few years at Hoover have been made all the richer by the presence of Jim Mattis. He is a man of great breadth—one who, as commander, advised his soldiers, 'Don't read handbooks; read great literature.' Jim struggles seriously with moral issues. He sees the importance of developing good strategies by identifying the best ideas about the subject at hand, always mindful that protecting one's values, whether personal or national, is essential."

This statement hints at the deep bond they developed, also shared with Harriet, that stretched broadly into many fields of interest. The three of them enjoyed many an evening at the Drell home discussing books, history, music, and other matters near and dear to their hearts and minds. Before Drell's death, Mattis described the great fondness he felt for both Sid and Harriet:

> After Secretary Shultz introduced us, Sid would often stop by my office at Hoover. Then I grew accustomed to having dinner with him and Harriet once a week when I was in town. Here's a great physicist, and here I am, from a completely different walk of life, with my three years of college and a fake PhD. My honorary PhD is from Washington College, the first school established after our revolution. So, Sid and I joke and smilingly call each other "Doctor."
>
> Sid and I work around the hall from each other in the "Shultz Corner" of Stanford's Hoover Institution. When Sid's office door opens, more than sunlight floods onto the second deck of Hoover! His booming voice and his sunny spirit light the neighborhood.

(L to R) Sid Drell, James Mattis, and George Shultz: three Hoover ("Shultz wing") notables, December 5, 2016.

I can even clearly hear the passion in his voice when he's on the telephone. Perhaps it's also a part of the loud-and-clear aspect of his beliefs. He's unafraid to call it as he sees it; if someone disapproves, they'll have to deal with it. Sid can assess the American political scene and call it for what it is. Still, he will listen to legitimate disagreement; he walks the middle road.

With all of his lofty achievements, one would think it would take humility to be a gentleman such as Sid is, but it doesn't. I have seldom used this word to define someone, but I think of Sid as valiant. I can imagine him on the bridge of a navy ship going into harm's way, just standing there ready, come what may. He's a warrior of lightness, not of doom and gloom. He's dealt with the most horrible weapons on Earth, but he's found a way to actually advance limiting them and ensuring safety. Perhaps some would expect that he'd be advocating "the bigger the megatonnage, the better." Not so. He recognizes danger because he applies such rigor to understanding every facet of nuclear weapons, and he'll fight for whatever he sees as necessary to keep us, and the world, as safe as possible from the dangers posed by them. He's a valiant guy. I've seen people who have put it all on the line; Sid is one of them. He will use a sword if he must, but he will do his best to construct better options.

Drell's Jason colleague and friend Richard Garwin expressed similar admiration for Drell's years of tireless service at the Hoover Institution: "For all these contributions, for his role as leader and exemplar—both technical and human—and for the pleasure it has given us to work with him over the decades, the national security community of the United States owes Sid Drell a great debt of gratitude. And in answer to the question, "National security—is there hope?" Garwin was reassuring: "There is, so long as people of Sid Drell's integrity and intelligence involve themselves in the battle."

James Goodby, an Annenberg Visiting Distinguished Fellow at the Hoover Institution since 2007, often joined Drell in the battle for national security over the course of many years. The two first met in Geneva in 1981 when Goodby, a career foreign service officer and specialist in nuclear weapons policy, was vice chairman of the US delegation to the Strategic Arms Reduction Talks (START). Earlier, in 1975, he had negotiated a new charter among the NATO allies and assisted as they negotiated the Helsinki Final Act of 1975. In 1993, Goodby was named chief US arms negotiator for the safe and secure dismantlement of nuclear weapons, a role in which he and his team successfully negotiated agreements with Russia, Kazakhstan, Belarus, and Ukraine to accelerate the elimination of nuclear weapons systems. Goodby offered some highlights of Drell's contributions to national security:

I would single out the Comprehensive Nuclear-Test-Ban Treaty [CTBT] as one of Sid's greatest accomplishments because of his sustained work in keeping it alive during a downtime. It was in 1993 that President Clinton decided—partially on the basis of Sid's advice—to extend the moratorium indefinitely. Congress had been considering another yearlong extension after the initial moratorium had ended. A review was in the works to determine if a permanent moratorium, which the president was considering, could be justified. Sid's direct interactions with Hazel O'Leary, secretary of energy at the time, were critical in the ultimate justification of a permanent moratorium. We can credit Sid for his important role in making that a reality. His contact with Hazel O'Leary and with John Shalikashvili helped seal the deal. Sid's conversations with then chairman of the Joint Chiefs of Staff Shalikashvili also led to the Joint Chiefs signing on to the president's position of permanence for the treaty. Regrettably, the CTBT was refused advice to ratify in 1999. It remains on the Senate's agenda.

We were exposed to many of Sid's ideas as a result of conversations that Shali [Shalikashvili], Sid, and I had at the State Department. Shali and I shared many of Sid's thoughts during our consultations with the Senate. Both of these extensive episodes are really of quite critical importance. They represent some highlights of national import in Sid's professional and governmental work.

I think of Sid as a very politically astute man who knew how to get things done—who was persistent and understood where and when to pull strings of power in order to make things happen. Sid's positions on issues added significant weight to the arguments he supported. He was often the essential counterweight to more cautious positions. His support frequently meant the difference between success or failure in negotiations that reduced nuclear dangers, And with the Jasons, one of the most important activities in his life for a very long time, he served as an accomplished leader of the group. Given their work, much of it secret, Sid was an effective go-between and facilitator of scientific brilliance in service to national security and of international significance.

In all, I would say that Sid deserves a great deal of credit for a lifetime of academic, scientific, and patriotic—as well as international—service. His legacy includes many highlights, but my choice of the most significant is his influence in the Nuclear-Test-Ban Treaty moratorium, still extant and holding. I am grateful for the personal ties we developed over the years; his presence in my professional and personal life was a real boon and continues to be an inspiration.

Sid and I wrote two books and one shorter publication together.[4] These were intense collaborations because Sid took the scientific approach to everything he did. We spent endless hours reviewing everything he or I wrote to ensure that it could be defended and that we had thought of the best arguments to propose for every issue we addressed. In each case, I believe the books were consequential—Sid always insisted on that as a goal—and they have stood the test of time. Together, these publications addressed nearly every issue governments need to consider as they ponder whether and how to reduce and eliminate the nuclear threat. I am grateful for the opportunity given to me to work with Sid on things such as these that matter.

The Gift of Friendship

As for the other man at the heart of this chapter in Drell's life, George Shultz spoke at length for this book about their friendship and collaboration:

---

4. The books are *A World Without Nuclear Weapons: End State Issues* (Stanford, CA: Hoover Institution Press, 2009) and *The Gravest Danger: Nuclear Weapons* (Stanford, CA: Hoover Institution Press, 2003). The shorter publication is *What Are Nuclear Weapons For?* (Washington, DC: Arms Control Association, 2007).

I think Sid's main gift to me was not so much his knowledge of nuclear matters as it was the friendship shared with a really wonderful human being. I would put a "capacity for friendship" at the top of the long list of Sid's many positive attributes. We didn't see eye to eye on every issue, but I think having contrasting philosophies and disagreeing on substantive issues are part of a profound bond.

One especially memorable moment between us happened in the wake of the symposium held at Hoover in September of 2016 to mark Sid's ninetieth birthday. Many colleagues and friends convened to hold forth on diverse topics of discussion that matched Sid's full and varied life to laud Sid, the scientist; Sid, the professor; Sid, the violinist; Sid, the husband and father; Sid, the humanist; and Sid, the connoisseur of Pappy Van Winkle bourbon. It was a moving event for all in attendance, but particularly for Sid. The following day, he confessed his reaction to it all, saying, "It was difficult for me. I never dreamed that I deserved that kind of praise, but I decided to sit back and take it."

After his retirement in 1998, Sid maintained offices at SLAC and Hoover, permanently settling at Hoover in 2015. Determined to make his time here constructive and meaningful, Sid never played the "I'm a big scientist from the lab" card. He simply wanted to be a positive influence. That desire was instinctive.

Some of my fondest memories are of the many mornings I would arrive at Hoover and see the lights on in Sid's office, located a few doors down the hall from my office. Stopping in for a visit with Sid was the ideal way to start a workday, and we would check in with each other to discuss whatever issues were on the top burner as the day progressed.

Sid lived his life fully, right up to the end. On December 19, 2016, the two of us held a conference to discuss strategic stability issues and Jim Timbie's suggested agenda for future meetings with Russian leaders. In addition to Timbie, others who attended the meeting included Jim Ellis, David Holloway, Bill Perry, and John Taylor. As an active participant in this discussion, held just two days before his death, Sid offered yet another lasting contribution to the national security dialogue.

Months earlier, in what would be his final in vivo efforts to focus attention on the urgency of eliminating nuclear weapons, Drell had joined George Shultz, Jim Goodby, and Raymond Jeanloz in a letter to the editor of the *New York Times*, "Imagining a World Without Nuclear Weapons," and then drafted a piece titled "What Are Nuclear Weapons For?" In the epilogue to this volume, Goodby and Jeanloz detail Drell's last at-bat with them in the nuclear security discussion, which continues posthumously, inspired by his legacy.

∿

CHAPTER 6

Bagatelles for Drell

D r. Sidney David Drell had a wealth of friends and chose a number of them to contribute to this project. Because some of the topics or contexts they touched upon either overlapped with other accounts or were not within the scope of previous chapter categories, we include them here. Contributors range from fellow physicists, Jasons, and public servants to journalists, an Episcopal bishop, and a neighbor of the Drells at the Vi retirement community in Palo Alto where Drell and his wife lived in his last years. The diversity of these tale-tellers and their perspectives are as expansive and charming as Sid was in gracing their lives.

As comments indicate, many of these stories were gathered when Drell was still living, while others were collected after his death. Each brings a welcoming sense of acquaintance with the warmth and inclusivity that Sid occasioned. All reinforce the significance of personal connections in the sum total of Drell's everyday life.

From the Fourth Estate

Philip Taubman is a former Moscow and Washington bureau chief and deputy editorial page editor at the *New York Times*. He served as secretary of the Stanford Board of Trustees and is now based at

Stanford's CISAC, where he is writing the first comprehensive biography of George Shultz. Drell features prominently in Taubman's 2012 book *The Partnership: Five Cold Warriors and Their Quest to Ban the Bomb*.[1] For this volume, Taubman offered glimpses of his long relationship with Drell.

I met Sid when I was a student at Stanford in the late 1960s. He was already known for his prominent role at SLAC and as a proponent of arms control as well as for being a force in nuclear threat reduction. As an undergraduate, I had a glancing acquaintance with him but didn't take any of his courses.

From my early acquaintance with Sid during my student days and throughout our many years of friendship, I have always been impressed by Sid's principled approach to his life and work. Passion, a trait often attributed to Sid, is indivisible from his principled view of what's right and wrong. An example of Sid's principled mindset and character was his eventual departure from Stanford's Center for International Security and Arms Control [CISAC], now the Center for International Security and Cooperation. The university leadership had not kept its word to him about whether faculty appointments would be allowed at CISAC, and when he discovered that they weren't to be permitted, he quit.

The most sustained and visible evidence of Sid's principled character, in my mind, is that of his relationship with Andrei Sakharov. It was quite extraordinary for him to defend Sakharov through all those years when he was silenced in the Soviet Union, including his internal exile. Most Americans, other than those in the scientific community or the defense field, would know Sid because of his defense of Sakharov.

In a certain sense, I would liken Sid to Sakharov. It's a very imperfect analogy; Sid did not have to dissent from government policy in a police state, nor was he sent into exile. But I think

---

1. New York: HarperCollins, 2012.

Sid's courage in exercising his convictions in his life and career is comparable to Sakharov's courage. Sid spoke up whenever he saw things that were not right, whether in government policy or Stanford programs. He was never afraid to say what he thought needed to be done.

In writing *The Partnership*, I had access to a great deal of biographical material, so I was made aware of the fact that Sid lived this kind of double life. At SLAC, he served as a physicist and later as deputy director. At the same time, he worked on classified technology projects and played a vital role in helping to develop a whole set of intelligence-gathering equipment that made a huge difference in keeping the peace. With Sid's help in technology development, some of the intelligence gathered allowed the United States to truly understand the extent of Soviet military strength and the Soviet nuclear threat. With the knowledge gained, we discovered what their capabilities were and could then go on to design a defense against those capabilities, not against any possibilities that could (but didn't) exist. Sid was a very important historical figure in developing and forging a transformational period in American intelligence. It signaled the time when we transitioned from a reliance primarily on human intelligence collection to a reliance on technical collection.

Through that development, called the Corona project, Sid worked with the giants of that era. They included Jim Killian, who served as Eisenhower's science adviser, and Edwin Land, founder of Polaroid and inventor of pre-digital instant photography, who was a vital adviser to the US government on technical intelligence collection. These were the titans of the midcentury, and there was Sid, a young man in the mix, already making a mark in this field.

An amusing anecdote reveals more of Sid the physicist. As I was researching the development of spy satellites for my book, I discovered that Sid had played an important role in satellite history. There were some very technical aspects to the book, and

I didn't feel confident writing about those matters in an accurate, knowledgeable way, so I asked Sid if he would go over the technical pages and give me some feedback. He very graciously agreed. When I was done with the manuscript, I sent him some of the technical material, including my rather impoverished effort to explain the physics of how a nuclear weapon works. He very dutifully and conscientiously read my stab at an explanation. His emailed response was three pages long and I could barely understand a word of it. I doubt Sid had ever dealt with someone as ignorant about physics as I was on technical and scientific matters.

Sid did so much for our country and really didn't get the credit he deserved for all those extraordinary accomplishments benefiting our nation. One great friendship borne from Sid's governmental, behind-the-scenes work is the Drell-Shultz alliance. Even when they authored that first op-ed for the *Wall Street Journal* in 2007, Sid insisted that he didn't want or need his name on it. Then, of course, we've seen close up the way George always wants to include Sid and ensure that the limelight is on Sid, along with the others.

In some ways, it's an unlikely friendship. If you know the two men, you understand it, but if you look at their lives—their political perspectives and so on—they're so very different that one's reaction is: Wow, that bond is interesting! Yet, they have found common ground on which to continue serving the public good, and they enjoy a solid, complementary friendship.

$$\sim\!\!\wedge\!\!\wedge$$

Washington Post journalist and former associate editor and chief foreign correspondent **Jim Hoagland** is the recipient of two Pulitzer Prizes for international reporting and commentary. Currently an Annenberg Distinguished Visiting Fellow at the Hoover Institution, he cowrote a 2015 *Foreign Affairs* article, "The Man Who Spoke Truth to Power: Andrei Sakharov's Enduring Relevance," with Drell and Shultz.

I've known Sid since I first became a Hoover fellow in 2010 through Hoover collaborations and through our mutual friendship with George. In 2014, we organized a Hoover conference on the legacy of Andrei Sakharov, the dissident Soviet physicist and human rights advocate for whom Sid and George shared a deep respect and admiration. After the conference, the three of us wrote a magazine piece summarizing the conference's findings. In addition, Sid and George jointly edited a book, *Andrei Sakharov: The Conscience of Humanity*, published by the Hoover Press in 2015, which contains a collection of insightful essays on Sakharov.

One of the adjectives I've used in describing Sid is "passionate." Another descriptor is "principled." He cares deeply about people and principles, and I have seen him defend both. At times, the adjective "fierce" is appropriate, too. He engages fiercely when he firmly believes that he is right, which he is, usually, in my experience. Sid is also very smart and has remarkable communication skills.

I characterize Sid's relationship with George Shultz as an example of an odd couple—odd in the ways that they differ but complement each other, making for a perfect match. It has been my pleasure to observe them closely in their work at Hoover and in their joint endeavor to alert the world to the enormous risks to human survival still posed by nuclear arsenals nearly three decades after the end of the Cold War.

From the Realm of Science

Lucy Shapiro, a professor of developmental biology and director of the Beckman Center for Molecular and Genetic Medicine at the Stanford University School of Medicine, is a recipient of the National Medal of Science, which she was awarded alongside Drell. Because she anticipated and worked for many years to educate her colleagues and peers about the probability of a pandemic, Shapiro could be characterized as the proverbial canary in the coal mine. In her years of acquaintance with Drell, she enjoyed many rewarding experiences, personally and professionally.

I first had the privilege of working with Sid on the President's Council of the University of California's National Lab Oversight group from 1993 to 1997. We dealt with an array of thorny issues facing the Livermore, Los Alamos, and Lawrence Berkeley national labs. Sid, as head of the council, led this group with deep insight, scientific breadth, tact, and vision. He could also quell the occasional rogue comment with a special look that spoke volumes.

It was in the mid-1990s that George Shultz initiated a small lunch group that has continued to meet monthly up to the present time. Invariably, there were four topics on the table: international and national news, items of concern to each of us at the moment, Stanford University, and finally, football. It was during these lunches that I first saw a playful aspect of Sid's usually highly analytical approach to problems. We enjoyed these lively, challenging, and deeply thoughtful lunch conversations. They also revealed a delicate balance in the close friendship between George and Sid, who sometimes had very different political viewpoints but always had enormous respect for one another.

Sid and Harriet were mainstays of a Stanford discussion group which includes several Stanford couples. The group has met each month during the academic year dating back over sixty years. One of our most memorable meetings featured Sid and Harriet's daughter Persis, then the director of SLAC, who discussed a particularly exciting technological advance.

In early 2013, each of our families joined us in Washington, DC, where Sid and I were to receive the National Medal of Science from President Obama. It was freezing cold on the day of the event, and Sid's mobility was somewhat compromised. As Sid and I left the hotel to board a government bus for the ride to the White House, Persis quietly asked me to look after her father.

When the bus approached the White House security entrance, Sid and I, in the front seats, noticed smoke rising from under the steering wheel. Remembering Persis's request, I told the driver to stop and open the door. Sid and I hustled off into the frigid air while everybody else stayed put. Shortly after our escape, we saw flames shooting up from the front of the bus. Sid simply said, "Let's get out of here!" That unnerving episode was quickly overshadowed by the joy of the award ceremony.

$$\mathcal{W}$$

Physicist **Malvin Ruderman** is known for his research in theoretical astrophysics, neutron stars, pulsars, the early universe, and cosmic gamma rays. A former professor of physics at the University of California–Berkeley, New York University, and Columbia University, he served as chair of Columbia's Department of Physics in the early 1970s. Ruderman, one of Drell's fellow Jasons, offered some fond memories of his friend.

Sid and I have been good friends and occasional collaborators in physics research ever since we became acquainted in 1950 when we were finishing our graduate degrees. We were one thousand miles apart—I was at Columbia University, Sid was at the University of Illinois—but in those days, graduate students in theoretical elementary particle physics usually knew each other.

I remember with great pleasure times that we worked together on some physics problems without a goal in mind, but mainly because the trip to find the answer was so enjoyable. An example was our accidental invention of a new way of giving small shoves to a satellite in space by pushing on a planetary magnetic field.

We named our process the Alfvén propulsion engine after the famous Swedish plasma physicist J. Alfvén. Our purposeful name came from the idea of putting its acronym, APE, together with the word "space," so that we could then propose an Ape in Space to join with the United States' famous Man-in-Space program. To my knowledge, our APE has never had an application.

$$\bigvee\!\!\bigwedge\!\!\bigwedge$$

Christopher Stubbs, experimental physicist, is dean of science at Harvard University, a professor in Harvard's department of physics, which he chaired from 2007 to 2010, and professor in the department of astronomy. His research focus is the interface between particle physics, cosmology, and gravitation. Stubbs is engaged in work on the construction of the Large Synoptic Survey Telescope, for which he was the inaugural project scientist. He is the founder of the Apollo collaboration, which employs lunar laser ranging and the earth-moon-sun system to search for novel gravitational effects. An Annenberg Distinguished Visiting Fellow at the Hoover Institution, Stubbs worked on reexamining a technical possibility for improving and updating technology for the Open Skies collection platforms.

Sid is a tremendous role model because he's an extremely capable theoretical physicist and has a statesmanship role in the security arena as a public intellectual.

If I had to choose one word to describe Sid, I'd say *integrity*. One especially informative moment for me was when, in the first few years of my work with Jason, I was asked to lead a study evaluating what was then a multibillion-dollar facility proposal for Los Alamos, one of the national weapons labs. It was a high-stakes Jason study. The technology and the politics of nuclear weapons were quite new to me at the time, and Sid took me under his wing and taught me how to approach thinking about that problem, broadly construed. At the end, we came out with a report that was actually very critical of the proposal; I'd like to think we helped save the taxpayers a very substantial amount of money. That, for me, was a particularly formative experience. I think it laid the foundation for a lot of our subsequent work together.

∿

Ellen Williams, distinguished university professor at the University of Maryland's Department of Physics, joined the Jason group thirty-three years after its formation. The focus of her scientific research has been surface properties and nanotechnology. Williams served as chair of the National Academy of Sciences committee on Technical Issues Concerning the Comprehensive Test Ban Treaty from 2009 to 2011 and was chief scientist at BP from 2010 to 2014. She was nominated by President Obama to be director of the Advanced Research Projects Agency–Energy, a position she held from December 2014 to January 2017. Williams was named a foreign member of the Royal Society (London) in 2016.

I have known Sid Drell since 1993, when I joined the Jason group. As a neophyte, and not being a member of the nuclear/high energy community, I had only a general knowledge of the US nuclear weapons program. But as I began to engage, I found Sid a rock of strength, supportive and welcoming in quiet mentorship and providing a phenomenal breadth of knowledge, both technical and political.

I saw Sid at work on stockpile stewardship issues, beginning with his leadership on the 1994 Jason report, "Science-Based Stockpile Stewardship." Although I'm sure there was much more going on behind the scenes, from my perspective that report was the opening shot in more than a decade of serious controversy—the question being whether it was possible to maintain the stockpile without nuclear testing.

It was a few years later when I began working directly with Sid, first on the Jason Signatures of Aging study. As a newcomer, I was startled to learn how little understanding had been developed (over all the years of the nuclear weapons program) about weapons' degradation as they aged and the effects of aging on performance. It seemed to me that testing fully assembled weapons had been the priority, overlooking potential aging issues with the assumption that new weapons would replace old ones.

Sid was an amazing mentor. His calm perspective and profound knowledge kept that study, and many studies with divisive issues to follow, on track. He worked tirelessly, always keeping the big picture in sight while the controversies raged over deeply detailed technical points. The fact that Sid was willing to take on such huge enterprises and remain committed throughout when he could easily have rested on his laurels is perfect testimony to his character.

From Arms Control Advocates

Strobe Talbott is a foreign policy analyst, former *Time* magazine journalist, and diplomat. He served as US deputy secretary of state from 1994 to 2001 and was president of the Brookings Institution from 2002 to 2017. Talbott had great respect and high praise for Drell's skills in diplomacy and in advocating for a particular cause.

I'd label Sid one of humanity's great enthusiasts. I can see him now, conversationally bouncing when he gets into a subject he cares a lot about.

Of distinction, too, is Sid's talent for debating, with great civility, Soviet scientists as well as people on the American side, to figure out rational ways to stave off the threat of nuclear war. There was something both stubborn and prescient about him. He would never give up in an argument, which doesn't mean that he would just stand his ground. Instead, he's one of those very rare people who can advocate for a position based on enormous technical knowledge but can also listen, thoughtfully and carefully, to those who hold other positions. And if Sid hears a valid point that he hadn't previously considered, he will incorporate that idea into a kind of variation of his basic views.

In communicating, he not only is an articulate transmitter of analysis, argument, and fact, but he also keeps his responder on. Not just a talker, he's very much a creative and attentive listener who is alert for things that will teach him something or stir him to rethink some line of his own views.

There's no question that Sid believed deeply in negotiated arms controls, but he was also very hardheaded about the need for diplomacy backed by force, recognizing the imperative of keeping a credible deterrent in the background while the US government tried to come to terms with the Soviets and then later the Russians.

Though Sid has a sunny disposition and is affable and collaborative in manner, it would be a real misfire to call him a dreamer. He was always extremely careful to ensure that profoundly ambitious goals for nuclear diplomacy could be achieved only through convincing the other side that their science, technology, and national security interests would all be taken into account. In other words, he was never in the clouds; he knew that to be a credible negotiator, it was essential to understand the other party's interests and capabilities and to respect them.

Sid can be counted in the number of world-class scientists who were able to master the wider and very complicated field of national and international politics, particularly the politics of the Cold War. In so doing, they could bring, along with their scientific expertise, a high degree of sophistication about the political realities.

With regard to Sid's life in physics, I recall a number of conversations with Pief Panofsky which made it obvious that he, as the titular superior, revered Sid, the titular deputy. I've never seen such an unusual regard held by a superior for a deputy, but clearly Sid deserved it.

$$\sim\!\!\wedge\!\!\wedge$$

Steve Andreasen was director for defense policy and arms control on the US National Security Council at the White House from 1993 to 2001. Currently, he teaches at the University of Minnesota's Humphrey School of Public Affairs and is a national security consultant to the Nuclear Threat Initiative. Andreasen met Drell while working on the Clinton-Gore transition team and on arms control and disarmament. Subsequently, he worked closely with Drell on the Comprehensive Nuclear-Test-Ban Treaty (CTBT) negotiations, the Stockpile Stewardship Program, nuclear test verification, missile defense, and related defense programs. Andreasen admired Drell's serious and measured approaches to matters of great importance, both national and personal in nature.

Sid combined passion with patience in a very practical, personal, and appealing way. He was passionate about issues, reducing nuclear risks being one of them, but other passions included music, his family, and human rights. And he approached these issues—including the many people he interacted with, both inside and outside of government—with great patience. He took time to discuss, illuminate, and explore issues and solutions, recognizing that progress often requires time and patience.

There were many memorable moments with Sid. They include planning sessions with him in the months leading up to the October 2006 conference, "Implications of the Reykjavik Summit on Its Twentieth Anniversary," hosted by Secretary Shultz at the Hoover Institution, and working with Sid in his office at SLAC on the day after that conference. The purpose of the gathering was to discuss how the Reagan-Gorbachev vision of a world free of nuclear weapons could be reinvigorated and reintroduced into US and global security policies. During this exciting and important time and effort, all of Sid's qualities—his ability to organize, think and write clearly, crystallize an argument, and make a passionate and persuasive case—were on full display. His contributions before, during, and after the Reykjavik conference were examples of those traits in action. Sid brought his usual rigor and patience to the effort as well as a keen understanding of the complexities involved.

As for his extraordinary professional achievements, I'd cite two examples. During the first Clinton term, when I was on the White House National Security Council staff, Sid was instrumental in defining US programs for stockpile stewardship and for enhancing our ability to verify a CTBT. He also played a key role with the Jasons in moving the administration to support a true "zero yield" CTBT.

In September 2016, my father, a Korean War veteran, and I published an op-ed piece on North Korea in the *Chicago Tribune*. Sid took the time to call and leave us an enthusiastic voice mail, complimentary as he always was: "Hey Steve! What a great column you and your father wrote. I'd like to talk to you about it. I'd like to think there was anybody near Washington or in the election these days who could take that wisdom and courage and do something with it. Please call. I'm home. Bye-bye." I've saved that voice mail—my last communication from him.

Raymond Jeanloz is a professor of Earth and planetary science and of astronomy at the University of California–Berkeley. He chairs the Committee on International Security and Arms Control at the National Academy of Sciences and has been an Annenberg Distinguished Visiting Fellow at Stanford's Hoover Institution since 2012. Jeanloz spoke of Drell's enviable suite of traits and his "three-way approach" that invariably brought success.

I've known Sid since the mid-1990s and have worked closely with him since then. Our efforts have combined technical and policy work for different parts of the US government or in advising the University of California system, the latter being in the context of the university's management of two of the nuclear weapons laboratories. Our collaborations have been that combination of technical analysis in a context of national security and, more generally, national policy issues.

I agree that passion is an absolutely typical "Sid" trait. I would say, though, that Sid possesses a rather unique mix of character traits, very much energized by that passion. I'll call it a "three-way blend" of (1) technical capability; (2) policy context—knowledge about policy, political issues in Washington, and the like; and (3) a broad moral, ethical stance based on a firm set of perspectives. Though that three-way approach isn't absolutely unique to Sid, it's certainly a Drell trademark. Required in this approach are an understanding of the technical aspects; a recognition of the realities of the political context, particularly in the United States; and a respect for the broader ethical-moral aspect that must inform or guide both policy and the recognition of the relevant technical issues.

In my opinion, Sid's characteristic three-way interaction in any collaboration is the dynamic that makes him very special to work with.

A memorable event for me, with Sid at the center, was SLAC's official retirement party for him. That daylong symposium was remarkable because it represented the different parts of Sid's life, career, and contributions as well as his personality as it played out in all of those realms. From his many technical contributions to his roles as a research physicist, professor, and mentor in the technical arena, Sid's achievements were recognized in great fashion by those who experienced them with him. Of course, there also was acclaim for his policy contributions, among them the congressional panel he chaired in the early nineties and his many years advising government and the national labs. All involved, in one way or another, stories of Sid's moral-ethical side and his choice of the right path to pursue. A matter of conscience was always very much at the forefront of Sid's thinking and actions while he pursued his fundamental goal of making the world a better place. In sum, at that retirement event, we witnessed the whole confluence of those traits in action throughout Sid's professional and personal life.

$$\backslash\mathcal{M}$$

James Timbie's association with Stanford and Sid Drell dates to 1966. A senior adviser at the US Department of State from 1983 to 2016, he played a key role in INF (Intermediate-Range Nuclear Forces) and START (Strategic Arms Reduction Treaty) nuclear arms–reduction negotiations and became known to some as "Drell's wingman." Timbie served as US technical expert in the nuclear agreements struck by the United States with Iran in 2015. He is currently an Annenberg Distinguished Visiting Fellow at the Hoover Institution.

I first came to Stanford in the fall of 1966 as a grad student in the physics department. At that time, Pief Panofsky was the director of SLAC. Panofsky, an experimental physicist, managed the construction of the accelerator and was in charge of experiments; Sid was the chief theoretician. It was during that period that Sid and bj Bjorken wrote the basic textbook on quantum field theory for our generation of physicists.

During the hiatus between completing work for my PhD in the fall of 1970 and graduation in April of 1971, I was contemplating what to do next and got involved in teaching the arms control class. The Vietnam War was on, so it was the most popular course at Stanford then, with hundreds of undergraduates attending. As a postdoc teaching assistant, I assisted John Lewis, Josh Lederberg, Pief, and Sid, who ran the course.

As I was considering ways to move ahead as a physicist, it gradually dawned on me that an interesting way forward would be to get involved in arms control. I approached Sid and Pief about this. Both were consultants to the Arms Control and Disarmament Agency, and they were instrumental in showing me the way.

Sid and Pief were quite a team; theirs was a complementary pairing that was highly effective and felicitous. They piqued my interest in the subject of arms control and the three of us had many inspiring conversations about the future. Then they helped to identify a position for me in the State Department. They introduced me to Spurgeon Keeny, who directed the part of the agency handling the initial stages of the strategic arms talks, including negotiations on the ABM Treaty. Sid and Pief put in a good word for me with Keeny and, after a lengthy process, the Arms Control Agency hired me as a physical science officer. Eventually, I went on to work for the deputy secretary of state.

Following the Reagan-Gorbachev meeting in Reykjavik in 1986 and the breakup of the Soviet Union, I played a major role in negotiations to remove nuclear weapons from Ukraine and to facilitate a project for the US to purchase highly enriched uranium that the Russians extracted from nuclear weapons they no longer needed. Once purchased, we would burn the uranium as fuel in US nuclear power stations. For twenty years, 10 percent of the electricity used in the United States derived from fuel originating in those Russian weapons. We had to develop elaborate means of verification that the material we were getting from the Russians actually came from highly enriched uranium from weapons; there was a lot of technical work involved.

From 1992 to 2013, when the last shipload arrived in the United States, it was an extensive, twenty-year project with plenty of ups and downs. In the end, it was a win-win because the Russians were able to get rid of a stockpile no longer needed, that material will never go back into weapons, and terrorists will not be able to get their hands on it. It was gratifying to be part of that effort from the very beginning to the very end.

From Friends and Admirers

William Swing, Episcopal bishop of California from 1980 to 2006, is the founder and president of United Religions Initiative, an organization dedicated to bridging cultural and religious differences in countries around the world. He has spent a lifetime in service to the homeless, the elderly, and the infirm. At the symposium held in honor of Drell's ninetieth birthday on September 13, 2016, Swing made the following remarks.

In the early 1980s, I invited three distinguished people to speak about nuclear weapons at Grace Cathedral [in San Francisco]. One was Cap Weinberger, then secretary of defense; another was McGeorge Bundy, an expert in American foreign and defense policy; and the third was Sidney Drell, a renowned physicist from Stanford University. That occasion was the start of my twenty-five-year friendship with Sid.

I would like to point out that Sid's ninetieth birthday comes at a moment when the attention of America falls on two matters of terror. Fifteen years ago, the 9/11 tragedy gouged great scars in New York, the Pentagon, and western Pennsylvania. Then, last week, North Korea tested its fifth nuclear device, sending shivers through Japan, South Korea, and the United States. From these two events, we learn that the intent to do cataclysmic harm is present today and the capacity for such harm is getting closer and closer. When I think about the threat, I also think about the qualities of sanity and humanity that are needed now. Both qualities are carried in Sid's heart and head.

I have a friend who was the chaplain to England's royal family. He loved to say, "The Queen Mother and I hate name-droppers." Even so, I mention to anyone who will listen, "Sid Drell and I like the same books." Most recently, he loaned me his books-on-tape edition of Herman Melville's *Moby-Dick*. Speaking of literature, when I write some little piece, Sid is always willing to give it a good read; only a friend would do that.

It is hard to mention Sid's name without mentioning the name of George Shultz. We have known great twosomes: Batman and Robin! Lum and Abner! But when I think of Sid and George, it's [Babe] Ruth and [Lou] Gehrig who come to my mind. They had clout, they were where the action was, and they were difference makers.

When my wife, Mary, and I are in need of good conversation and a good meal, we plot an invitation for dinner with Harriet and Sid. Time with them is always a grace note in our lives.

$$\sim\!\!\wedge\!\!\wedge$$

Fred Rehmus, Stanford MBA 1961, is a recipient of Stanford's Gold Spike Award in recognition of his many years of volunteer activity at Stanford University, including the Cantor Arts Center, the Graduate School of Business Alumni Association Board of Directors, and the Stanford Alumni Association. As one of the Drells' neighbors at the Vi retirement community in Palo Alto, Rehmus had several sweet moments to reveal.

Sid and I bonded through a peculiar shared interest in high-quality bourbon whiskey. Ours was a ten-year competition of trying to outdo each other by offering our candidate for the title of best bourbon. The process gave us an opportunity to spend a lot of time in conversation. Mind you, we're quite abstemious, and it's rare that we drink more than a full ounce in our tastings. It isn't simply the economics of it; it's a matter of providing a way for us to get together frequently to discuss and decide on answers to the world's problems, as well.

My friendship with Sid is on a very different level from his professional relationships. We were ships passing in the night who seemed to like the way we were handling the sails and developed a fairly deep relationship. It's also rather convenient—we just have to walk down the hall to see each other.

Sid is a very good friend whom I love dearly and respect highly. Though I know little about his professional background, anything I've picked up has been almost incidental in terms of broader conversations. But because of Ann Finkbeiner's book, *The Jasons*, I'm also aware of Sid's role in the extraordinary input from the top scientific minds in the country who address the nation's most serious scientific problems.

Sid's a polymath, you know. He not only has a career in academia, but this man is a remarkable student of music and of literature. And while his politics may be suspect, he's a wonderful guy to converse with. We enjoy each other's company.

\/\/\

James Ellis Jr., a retired four-star admiral and former commander of the US Strategic Command, was president and chief executive officer of the Institute of Nuclear Power Operations from 2005 to 2012. He has been an Annenberg Distinguished Visiting Fellow at the Hoover Institution since 2013. In 2016, he joined in the Hoover-sponsored event honoring Drell on his ninetieth birthday, where he made the following statement.

My theme in the few minutes allotted me on this grand occasion is simply to address the word "service" in the human terms that Sid so well demonstrates. For me, service is a mirror image of the motto of my Naval Academy class of 1969, *non sibi*—not for self. It's part of the mission statement for each of the other three service academies, and, as I sometimes note, service academies are so named for a reason.

In Sid Drell's case, the word is twice mentioned in the informal motto of his beloved Princeton University: "Princeton in the nation's service and the service of humanity." Service is also a part of the founding charter of the great university where we gather today—and where Sid continues to serve—defined in the 1885 Stanford founding grant as "to promote the public welfare by exercising an influence in behalf of humanity and civilization." No words better characterize Sid Drell's service to the nation than those.

Dr. Martin Luther King Jr. defined service as "the rent we pay for the space we occupy in the world." But I wager that Sid would urge us to think of service not as a cost or a price or a sacrifice but as a gift that, if freely and honestly given, will be repaid many times over. Sid Drell has been fortunate enough to have those opportunities in abundance. But his service reminds us mortals that all of us can serve, wherever we find ourselves, in ways large and small, in or out of uniform, while defining our personal leadership style along the way, because true, honest, and selfless service, in my view, is the essence of leadership.

Now, Sid might protest that he doesn't see himself as a leader, but I know that all of us in this room would violently disagree. We've already had the debate on his style of management. I would argue that management and leadership are both essential, but they are not at all the same. One manages things, but one leads people. The finest leaders I ever knew did not simply occupy the front-row chairs in the fighter squadron ready room or settle into the captain's chair on the bridge at the head of the battalion or, as now, sit in the C-suite corner offices of the academic halls of power. Real leaders instinctively know that their job is to give their direct reports everything they need to succeed—training, guidance, resources, vision, inspiration, mentoring, patient leadership, and support—especially when those they lead make honest mistakes and come up short, as all of us inevitably will. Over six decades, Sid has met all of those duties and more.

In Sid's Own Words

James Goodby and Raymond Jeanloz

Since Sid Drell's passing, a new American administration has sought to nullify the legacy left by the Obama administration. Relative to the issue of nuclear policy—the challenging arena Sid regarded as a crucial one to continue addressing—that legacy held still less than Sid had hoped for. In the final months of his life he began to write about those lost opportunities and the ensuing dangers of more losses to come. His thoughts, typically, were based on the realities of nuclear weapons that he knew so well and on his hope that some opening to a better world—one in which policy makers and public interest can regain prominence in addressing the elimination of dangers posed by nuclear weapons—could ultimately offer a springboard to a cascade of actions reducing the nuclear threat.

Perhaps the last of Sid's hundreds of essays written or cowritten to influence public opinion appeared as a letter to the editor in the *New York Times* on April 15, 2016. With George Shultz and other colleagues contributing, the letter reiterated Sid's vision of a world without nuclear weapons and pointed out that creating the conditions for feasible nuclear reductions was both a political task and a technical one. This theme was later picked up by President Obama, who, on May 27, 2016, became the first US president to visit Hiroshima. On that occasion, the president said, "Technological progress without an equivalent progress in human institutions can doom us. The scientific revolution that led to the splitting of an atom requires a moral revolution as well."

The letter to the editor of the *New York Times*, printed below, was blunt in pointing out that "the goal of eliminating the nuclear threat to humanity will continue to be remote so long as nuclear weapons and their delivery systems remain unconstrained for seven of the nine states that have nuclear weapons and the other two have no further negotiations continuing or planned."

Drell, of course, hoped for a joint enterprise of many nations to be created, its goal to reintroduce nuclear reductions into the center of the international agenda. A joint enterprise such as he envisioned remains one of the major challenges to the nations of the world. It would take into account the fact that any treaty to ban nuclear weapons that does not specify *how* their elimination might be achieved will not bring us closer to a world free of nuclear weapons. Establishing the joint enterprise that Sid envisioned is an essential step in any project aimed at reducing the nuclear threat to humanity.

The full text of the letter follows.

Imagining "a World Without Nuclear Weapons"

New York Times, April 15, 2016

To the Editor:
"From Hiroshima to a Nuke-Free World" (editorial, April 13) underscored the need for "bolder action" than the Obama administration has been able to take in recent years to move toward its long-term goal of a world without nuclear weapons, a vision that we share.

The goal of eliminating nuclear weapons can be achieved only by creating the conditions that would make nuclear reductions feasible, a political task as well as a technical one, and many countries must work together in a joint enterprise to accomplish this.

The fourth Nuclear Security Summit, held in Washington this month, was a solid achievement, but the goal of eliminating the nuclear threat to humanity will continue to be remote so long as nuclear weapons and their delivery systems remain unconstrained for seven of the nine states that have nuclear weapons and the other two have no further negotiations continuing or planned.

Even the levels agreed between the United States and Russia in the New Start treaty are higher than necessary for a prudent deterrent strategy.

Your editorial rightly focused on individual steps that could be taken now to rekindle the flame of hope that briefly flared during the first years of this administration. Strengthening the moratorium on explosive tests of nuclear devices and agreeing to stop production of fissile materials for use in bombs and missile warheads would be valuable steps in rebuilding momentum toward nuclear weapons reductions to the levels of 1,000 each for the United States and Russia, as President Obama suggested in a speech in Berlin.

George P. Shultz
James E. Goodby
Sidney D. Drell
Raymond Jeanloz

Stanford, Calif.

Drell's attention in those final months was also focused on US nuclear deterrent strategy. He returned to a theme he had written about before: What are nuclear weapons for? Sid was convinced that the utility of nuclear weapons in international security policy needed to be reexamined from time to time as technology advanced and global conditions changed. That conviction is relevant today and will remain so despite changes in leadership in the United States and elsewhere.

On July 25, 2016, Drell sent an email to his colleagues labeled a "first rough draft" of his views of how nuclear weapons should be fitted into US deterrent strategy. Despite being a rough draft, it merits the attention of those in power in Washington today.

What Are Nuclear Weapons For?

In view of the terrible consequences of the use of nuclear weapons, the United States should make it clear that as matters now stand, every vital interest beyond deterring nuclear attack on the US and/or our allies can be met by maintaining conventional readiness. There is no visible case at present that could require the United States to be forced into making a choice between defeat and the first use of nuclear weapons. This perspective must be maintained as we look ahead at future challenges.

However, we must recognize that this situation could change, requiring us to make such a dreadful choice of using nuclear weapons in an actual strike. As a result of rapid developments in new technologies, we must respond to and prepare to preserve the present situation with high priority in order to provide a barrier to facing such a choice. Some of these technologies are robots, artificial intelligence, managing cyber advances, nano-energetics, drones, space weapons, three-dimensional manufacturing, and the handling of huge quantities of data.

We must face the fact that it is not only other large nuclear countries that at present are growing threats, enabled by new smaller, smarter, and cheaper sensors. We also have to be concerned with smart, and perhaps suicidal, individuals for whom nuclear deterrence has no real value.

Is there any alternative to a nuclear response to a nuclear attack on the US? This depends upon the source as well as the size of a nuclear attack. If it is a deliberate nuclear attack, one has to weigh the casualties it caused and the policies of the opponent who relied on such weapons. But there need not be a nuclear response as a blanket response statement. If it is a very limited strike, one may do comparable damage and devastation with conventional weapons. As a requirement for planning future force structures, we should be confident that our non-nuclear response will still be effective against the potential defenses of the attacker.

What is the value of a rapid response to an attack? Again, it must be weighed on the size of the initial attack, the behavior and the potential for further retaliation, and the goal of the opponent. This analysis will require at least a pause to try to figure out the nature of the attack and the strategies behind it and to determine an appropriate technically balanced response.

Is there any way to determine realistically what it means to prevail in a nuclear war? No. If a nuclear war starts and is quickly stopped, when people realize the danger to civilization and life itself as we know it, we may survive. But without limits, given the existing mega-tonnage and recognizing that we have no data or experience to tell us what it would take to credibly stop a nuclear war, if we fail to stop it quickly one has to accept the fact that we may well be ending life on Earth and our civilization.

Finally, Drell turned his attention to a matter he had addressed before in *Reducing Nuclear Danger: The Road Away from the Brink*, a book he wrote in 1994 with McGeorge Bundy and Admiral William Crowe.[1] The book covered matters concerning declaratory policy for

1. Washington, DC: Brookings Institution Press.

the potential use of nuclear weapons by the United States. This issue had particular resonance in 2018 in light of a nuclear weapons crisis in Northeast Asia and a possible second crisis with regard to Iran. Composed with two of his closest colleagues, the writing (drawn from ideas presented in the book) was an attempt to describe how nuclear deterrence policy should be applied in today's circumstances. Dated October 10, 2016, the following outline for a longer piece may have been Sid's last effort to show the limits of nuclear weapons in achieving American national security objectives.

On Deterrence in US Defense Policy

Sidney Drell, James Goodby, and Raymond Jeanloz

Deterrence is an essential element of US defense policy. The prevention of activities inimical to the security and well-being of the American people and US allies and friends must always be at the forefront of US national security policy. If deterrence by all available and relevant means should fail, then the United States must be prepared to respond in appropriate ways to redress the situation. The use of military force is a key component of both deterrence and of a response in the event of a failure to deter in cases that are rooted in military actions by an adversary, including a response to a cyber-attack.

The threatened use of nuclear weapons by the United States is an element of US national security policy so long as nuclear weapons remain in the hands of potential adversaries. The United States will not use or threaten to use nuclear weapons against non-nuclear weapon states that are party to the Nuclear Non-Proliferation Treaty (NPT) and in compliance with their nuclear non-proliferation obligations. The United States will seek action by the UN Security Council to provide assistance in the event that a country is threatened or attacked with nuclear weapons.

The United States has close alliances, formal or informal, with a number of nations that count on the United States to buttress their defense with nuclear weapons, if necessary, as a last resort. So long as the United States and its allies agree that a prudent defense posture requires a nuclear component, the United States must reserve the right to initiate the use of nuclear weapons if all other means of deterrence or defense have failed.

For many years, the primary purpose of the US nuclear arsenal has been to deter the use of nuclear weapons by potential adversaries, reserving the use of nuclear weapons for last-resort situations. This remains US policy while the United States works with all nations to create the conditions for a world without nuclear weapons. The United States also intends to strengthen the non-nuclear elements of its national deterrence posture and to assist its friends and allies in doing so.

For Sid

Yet another form of loving tribute comes full circle. Mourning the untimely loss of his beloved colleague Amos de-Shalit, Drell offered these words: "My fellow research associate for Viki Weisskopf at MIT and beloved friend thereafter, died in 1969 at the age of 42 midst a brilliant career as physicist, educator, and humanist at the Weizmann Institute—yet another young tragic death of a prince!"

Accompanying the text of his eulogy for de-Shalit was one of Sid's keepsakes—words written by Albert Einstein to Dr. Otto Juliusburger in 1947: "People like you and me, though mortal of course, like everyone else, do not grow old no matter how long we live. . . . We never cease to stand like curious children before the great Mystery into which we are born."[1]

And then, when the time came for us to process our own grief over Drell's final world-stage exit, there was solace to be found as we imagined the freeing of his spirit, now distilled to the elemental, to

---

1. From Helen Dukas and Banesh Hoffmann, eds., *Albert Einstein, the Human Side: New Glimpses from His Archive* (Princeton, NJ: Princeton University Press, 1979), 82.

joyride the great enigma of Time's arrow. His lifetime's youthful curiosity was spent in scientific high energy quests to unravel the great mystery of time and the elementary sources of the cosmos.

Time's Arrow

You ride Time's Arrow
now, and differently,
fundamentally significant
as man can be;

finished with this earthly iteration,
merged in nature's transubstantiation
of dynamic recipe
for distribution to whatever was-is-might be.

How rich, the Drell incarnation:
promise fulfilled, the bestowed applied;
success earned in principled stride,
a life in service exemplified.

For you no tomb, bier
or loamy barrow—
your constancy here in legacy
broad as Fermat's Margin too narrow.

For physicists, Time sleuths born and bred,
there's special place, it's said,
for delving and surmising
elementary truths for prising
in time's yeasty bread.

And so,
remaining vital as physics' house sparrow,
off now, *you*,
to ride Time's arrow!

Lenora Ferro
Portola Valley, California, 2017

Acknowledgments

To all who participated in this effort, we owe several magnitudes of appreciation: first, for their generosity, both personal and professional; second, for the contributions they themselves, individually and collectively, made to the historic events noted herein; third, for the examples set as they tendered their extraordinary bests while remaining true to the highest of principles—singularly and in accordance with the scientific method that guards and guides as a beacon of probity; and, finally, for the magnificence they unleashed as exemplars whose legacies will grow in time, prompting others to their own heights of possibility—à la Drell. We are profoundly grateful to each of these individuals, listed below.

The experiences garnered in acquaintance with Sid and the lifetime of memories he suggested for this project, as well as the opportunities to learn about the daily work of physicists who have produced earth-shattering and cosmic-revealing developments, have been life altering for us. We could have hoped for no greater gift than to have the opportunity to foster widespread recognition befitting Sidney Drell and the remarkable band of Drell friends and colleagues who people these pages.

And our thanks go particularly to James Bjorken, aka "bj," whose help with physics questions and some details of historic significance went beyond the call of duty. When the project was in its infancy, we asked Sid to nominate a proxy—someone we could trust for answers and suggestions concerning matters we hoped to keep secret from our subject as a surprise to be sprung only after Sid could hold the finished book in his hands. That proxy, who remained vital until the finish line, was bj. So to him we owe a special debt of gratitude for his generosity and kindness in answering queries of all sorts and in making suggestions as we'd requested. Bj's significance in Sid's life as a former student, colleague, and friend was clear. We feel fortunate to have had benefit of his trusted counsel and friendship. It should be added here that bj's name was often on the lips of others who offered their tales to this effort, extolling him as the *ne plus ultra* of Sid's contributions as a teacher, mentor, and colleague in physics and as a friend and extended family member.

It was a pleasure to work with Chris Dauer and the staff of the Hoover Institution Press. The professionalism of Danica Hodge, Alison Law, Barbara Arellano, and Barbara Egbert was matched by their creative approach to producing this book.

Finally, we deeply appreciate the support of Secretary George Shultz, who oversaw and encouraged our efforts to bring this book to fruition. As one whom Sid regarded as a significant catalyst for the many successes the two orchestrated in matters of national and international import, Shultz looms large in Drell's life, and thus in this history, which he shepherded.

Contributors:

Steve Andreasen	David Hamburg	Joel Primack
James "bj" Bjorken	Haim Harari	Fred Rehmus
Richard Blankenbecler	J. Bryan Hehir	Burton Richter
Lance Dixon	Jim Hoagland	Malvin Ruderman
Daniel Drell	David Holloway	Lucy Shapiro
Harriet Drell	Boris Ioffe	George Shultz
Joanna Drell	Robert Jaffe	Hu Side
Persis Drell	Raymond Jeanloz	Charles Slichter
Sidney Drell	Joyce Kobayashi	Christopher Stubbs
James Ellis Jr.	James Mattis	William Swing
Richard Garwin	George Miller	Strobe Talbott
Fred Gilman	Hazelle Miloradovitch	Philip Taubman
James Goodby	Mark Moynihan	James Timbie
Deborah Gordon	William Perry	Ellen Williams
Rose Gottemoeller	Bob Peurifoy	Tung-Mow Yan

Sidney D. Drell's Awards and Honors

2015 Dwight D. Eisenhower Award, shared with George Shultz, presented by the American Nuclear Society

2013 University of Illinois College of Engineering Hall of Fame induction

2012 Reykjavik Award, shared with Rose Gottemoeller, presented by the Federation of American Scientists

2012 Federation of American Scientists Public Service Award, shared with George Shultz, William Perry, Sam Nunn, and Henry Kissinger

2012 Gold Medal of Excellence presented by the National Nuclear Security Administration

2011 National Medal of Science

2010 Annual Sidney D. Drell Achievement Academic Award created by the Intelligence and National Security Alliance for graduate students and untenured professors

2008 Rumford Prize, shared with Sam Nunn, William Perry, and George Shultz, presented by the American Academy of Arts and Sciences

2005 Heinz Award for Public Policy

2001 William O. Baker Award presented by the Intelligence and National Security Alliance

2001   National Intelligence Distinguished Service Medal
        presented by the director of Central Intelligence

2001   Honorary doctoral degrees awarded by Tel Aviv
        University and the Weizmann Institute of Science

2000   Heinz R. Pagels Human Rights of Scientists Award,
        shared with Lin Hai, presented by the New York
        Academy of Sciences

2000   The Enrico Fermi Award, shared with Sheldon Datz
        and Herbert F. York, presented on behalf of the
        president and the secretary of energy

2000   Founder of National Reconnaissance as a Space
        Discipline Award, shared with nine other scientists,
        presented by the US National Reconnaissance Office

2000   University of California Presidential Medal

1999–2000 Linus Pauling Medal of Stanford University

1998   I. Ya. Pomeranchuk Prize, shared with A. I. Akheizer,
        presented by the Institute of Theoretical and
        Experimental Physics, Moscow

1997   Distinguished Associate Award presented by the US
        Department of Energy

1996   Gian Carlo Wick Commemorative Medal, World
        Federation of Scientists

1995   John P. McGovern Science and Society Medal
        presented by Sigma Xi

1994   Ettore Majorana-Erice-Science for Peace Prize,
        shared with the late Linus Pauling, presented by
        the Ettore Majorana Center for Scientific Culture

1994   Woodrow Wilson Award presented by Princeton
        University

1993   Hilliard Roderick Prize presented by the American
        Association for the Advancement of Science

1988   University of Illinois Alumni Achievement Award

1984–89 John D. and Catherine T. MacArthur Foundation
        Fellowship

1983   Natural Resources Defense Council honoree

1981   Honorary doctoral degree awarded by the University
        of Illinois

1980   Leo Szilard Award for Physics in the Public Interest
        presented by the American Physical Society

1979–80 Lewis M. Terman Professor and Fellow, Stanford
        University

1978   Richtmyer Memorial Lecturer, American Association
        of Physics Teachers

1973   Alumni Award for Distinguished Service in
        Engineering presented by the University of Illinois

1972   Ernest Orlando Lawrence Memorial Award presented
        by the US Atomic Energy Commission

1971–72 Guggenheim Fellowship

1961–62 Guggenheim Fellowship

Image Credits

Note: Letters refer to pages in the photo section.

Drell collection: 2, 4, 9, 24, 31, 34, A, B (top and middle), D (top), E, G (bottom)

Doug Menuez: C (top)

Harley McAdams: F (bottom)

Harvey L. Lynch: 89, 96, 105

Hoover Institution composite from Drell and Shultz collections: D (bottom)

J. R. Garappolo and C. G. Pease © Light at 11B: 110

Liza Semyonov: 86

NASA/JPL-Caltech: H

National Science & Technology Medals Foundation/Ryan K. Morris: F (top)

SLAC Archives: frontispiece, xii, 42

SLAC Archives, Mike Wood photo: B (bottom)

Stanford News Service/Chuck Painter: 50

Stanford University, Department of Special Collections and University Archives, Box: 21, Folder: Faculty housing—Alvarado Row—#2, https://purl.stanford.edu/pk314hr6771: 13

Stanford University, News Service, Records (SC0122), https://purl.stanford.edu/kq970kro418: 47

Susan Southworth: 115

The White House: 58, 70, C (bottom), G (top)

About the Authors

With Paris as backdrop to their introduction decades ago, it was happenstance that the collaborators in this effort had defected from their original educational backgrounds and experiences (from psychology and law to English literature and art history), choosing instead to blend interests that eventually brought them to a professional partnership in the world of writing. Their efforts since have been in collecting and setting pen to the truths and wonders of subjects such as Sidney Drell, whose example and lifetime contributions instruct and inspire.

For **Lenora Ferro**, local writer, the ideal goal for the art and craft of writing is as means to explore, learn, capture, and bring to light—through one storied life or culture at a time—the inevitably universal sacred in the ordinary . . . and vice versa.

In her professional life, **Susan Southworth** has worked with nationally and internationally renowned public figures and has been both an aide-de-camp to former secretary of state George Shultz and a prized editor for professionals in varied fields of expertise.

Index